On the Road to
Renewal

A Practical Approach to Problems

Clara M. van Dijk

Importantia Publishing

www.importantia.com

Copyright © 2008 C.M. van Dijk, the Netherlands

Original title: *Pastorale tips voor iedereen*, 1992 published by Stg. Moria, Amstelveen, the Netherlands. Republished under the title *Op weg naar vernieuwing* by Importantia Publishing (2008).

Translated by the author, with corrections by Mrs. Claire Rothrock-Hale.

Copyright for this book-edition: © 2008 Importantia Publishing

Importantia Publishing
P.O. box 9187
3301 AD Dordrecht
The Netherlands

www.importantia.com

ISBN 978 90 5719 161 9

This book is also available in the Mobipocket and Online Bible ebook formats (www.onlinebible.org)

All rights reserved. No part of this publication may be reproduced or transmitted in any form without the prior permission in writing from the publisher.

TABLE OF CONTENTS

FOREWORD	5
AN INTRODUCTION THAT CANNOT BE SKIPPED	7
1 HOW CAN WE FACE SUFFERING?	12
2 WHEN WE FEEL DOWN-HEARTED OR DEPRESSED	32
3 DEALING WITH THE FEAR OF MAN	50
4 ADVICE ON INSECURITY	63
5 WHAT TO DO ABOUT LOW SELF-ESTEEM	76
6 IN SEARCH OF OUR IDENTITY	96
7 FROM LONELINESS TO RELATIONSHIPS	109
8 HANDLING PROBLEMS IN RELATIONSHIPS	128
9 LONGING FOR RENEWAL	156
APPENDIX	176
TOPICAL REGISTER	196
RECOMMENDED BOOKS	200

FOREWORD

There is a Dutch saying, "Good advice is costly". Costly and precious - not because of a price tag, but because of the battle and deep experiences from which we learn those precious lessons.

That has been true in my life. It often seemed as if no books were written for my problems - but wasn't it true that the answers had to be there in God's Word? Diligently I searched for solutions and was very careful to note any advice I found. A pencil and paper were right next to my pillow at night, so that "special" thoughts and insights could be quickly jotted down: insights from a Bible passage or creative thoughts that could help me in my battles. For many years, I carefully wrote down everything that seemed useful: advice from God's Word, from sermons and Bible studies, conversations with friends, or from pastoral studies that showed me, for instance, what "renewal of the mind" meant, or how important it is to forgive. Several of the books mentioned in the Bibliography have also meant a lot to me, and the courses in pastoral counseling by Youth With A Mission have been most instructive!

We learn not only from other people's battles: friends who share from their wisdom, or people in the Bible like Joseph that inspire us, but God also wants us to learn from Him directly, by having an open ear to what He has to say to us when we face a difficult situation. That is the most precious counsel of all! If we guard His answers and advice as a precious treasure, we can accumulate our own list with His counsel, especially for our situation and trials: new insights, comforting words, and guideposts for our personal lives, as a source of strength and encouragement from above. Those precious life lessons are like divine sparks that we treasure within our hearts, without losing sight of the Source - God

Himself. Our true help lies in a prayerful relationship with Him.

In counseling others, the same sort of Biblical principles and guidelines kept coming up when sharing advice. By writing down these principles and experiences, I hope to allow a broader group of people to benefit from them. Isn't it wonderful, that our trials and problems can actually help others, so that they do not need to "reinvent the wheel"...

In order to make the contents of this book more accessible to those who have English as a second language, difficult words have been avoided. Furthermore, the style is kept compact to keep this book within the financial reach of many.

I am grateful both to the Lord and to those around me for all these insights and ideas; I have found these to be of great value throughout life's trials.

I do thank all those who have read these chapters for their helpful comments, especially Ir. P.N. Ruige from Velp, the Netherlands, for much appreciated advice and encouragement while this book came into being. Invaluable have been the prayer warriors that I am privileged to call my friends. Last, but not least, my deep gratitude goes out to Mrs. Claire Rothrock-Hale, who corrected the English translation.

Clara M. van Dijk

Spring 2002.

AN INTRODUCTION THAT CANNOT BE SKIPPED

Making the most of your life...

Many of us hope that our personal life can make a difference in this world, being like salt and a shining light (Matth.5:13-16), and that we may learn how to help others. However, much of our energy is often spent on our own busy life and our daily problems, and this book tries to be of help in removing these obstacles so that we can take our focus off these.

Yet no book can ever be a substitute to the help that Jesus Himself wants to give us, and many of us may spend too little time sitting at Jesus' feet like Mary did (Lk.10:42). For *"only one thing is needful"*: to be close to Jesus and take time to enjoy His love. He will teach and guide the meek in His way (Ps.25:9). The Marthas of this life may jump to this book, while the Marys may only see it as one of many occasional tools - and they are right. Knowing Jesus and spending time with Him will be of much more help in dealing with our problems than any "how-to" book ever could. If you are not convinced of this, it will be better not to focus on this book but to start spending more time with Jesus and His Book of books. By focusing on Him as the goal of our heart, we will truly make the most of our life!

So - the present booklet can be no more than an imperfect tool, to be used in times of heartache or hardship. Most of us do not seek answers for "heavy" problems such as drug abuse and divorce, for which more professional help is needed than this book can give. However, the normal daily troubles may eat up all of our courage and energy, especially in the area of our feelings, so that we don't have much energy left to give to others. Even as Christians, we may not always find a good counselor to encourage us and to give us a new perspective on things.

That is the goal of this booklet: to be a road-mark to advice from the Bible, to help us, as God's army, to deal with our battles and to prepare us for the true battle for His Kingdom. That way, it helps to make the most of our lives! Many a Christian around us could function better in trials, if they were handed the spiritual tools for that (Is.40:3-5; 57:14; Eph.6:10-18; Heb.12:2). For there are indeed Biblical answers, often not even hard ones! Isn't it wonderful, that God's advice to us humans is truly accessible? The Bible itself gives the best advice ever written and, therefore, many helpful Bible references are given so that the readers can look these up and see the *context* that may give a clearer picture.

Doing something about it

This small book may be used for reference rather than as a book to read through in a cursory manner - even though chapters on related topics are placed together. This is intended for those who have problems in a certain area and who want to look up some advice in a related chapter (see also the Table of Contents, the Topical Register and the Appendix).

However, this will only help if we truly want to *do* something about it. Not all chapters or every advice here may be of help; *they are not laws*! Only the Word of God has true authority, as a lamp to our feet and a light to our path (Ps.119:105). Again and again, we may let the Word speak to our hearts, and as we act upon that we lay the only true foundation for the house of our lives (Mt.7:24).

Perhaps some of the advice in this book may not strike a chord with you. The counsel that would have helped you may not be found here, and not every advice is applicable to everybody's situation. We all have our own personality and approach, our own unique situations. It is better to only use just such advice as appeals to you, that which seems practical and gives you peace or even joy. Such advice may clearly apply to your situation or be in line with what seems helpful to you at this time in your life. You can then lay aside other chapters until you see a benefit from those; yet do apply those insights that are "useful" for your own daily life and take them seriously - they may help indeed. Use them prayerfully, ask God about them. Human counsel itself is limited, and God is so much greater than we ask or think; His ways are so much higher than ours (Eph.3:20; Is.55:9). Without Him, any advice may become a law or system, in which there is no salvation! Salvation is in no one else but Jesus Christ, in the riches of His grace and through the forgiveness of our sins (Ac.4:12; Col.1:13-14; Eph.1:7).

In a living prayer relationship with Him, we find the wonderful Counselor who died for our sins (no room for guilt), who rose from the dead (giving new life), who sent the Comforter to you and me (a very present help in trouble), and who prepares a place for us in heaven (hope for the future). He Himself wants to encourage us!

Often, we are not in difficult circumstances, have no great challenges ahead of us, and just feel that vague desire for more... then, too, some of these words may help. Yet, whatever we try to do, we need God and can quietly walk behind the Good Shepherd. We can be relaxed in our contact with Him, not as "workaholic Christians" but as prayerful Christians, knowing that we are secure with the heavenly Father.

One of the Dutch readers said, "do not worry if you are doing everything right. The Shepherd can give you a correction with His staff when you really are about to go the wrong way. Should you not notice the Good Shepherd as much - because you are busy grazing while avoiding thorns and rocks and the pushing of other sheep and those nasty barking dogs - you may still be convinced that you belong to the flock. Be convinced that He still wants to find for you the greenest pastures in the area. We do not need to walk ahead of Him, but may continue grazing. We do not need to strain our thoughts on 'how to have a perfect life of faith' - like a child that continually says to his father, 'Look how well I play with my friends', rather than just playing and being immersed in that. Fathers can immensely enjoy that. That normal life is God's precious gift!"

Helpful guidelines

When seeking counsel, it may help to first read through the guidelines below. They form the basis for this book and come up in almost every chapter. In themselves, these give a perspective in which we may find solutions more quickly. In the Appendix, these guidelines are worked out in more detail (also, the Topical Register may help you to find more on the theme of your choice.)

While reading, simply ask yourself, "what guideline can be of help in my personal situation?""

These guidelines are:
1. Stand in the "first love" to the Lord, spending time with Him. (Rev.2:4)
2. Maintain a living prayer relationship with Him.
3. Strive for deep obedience to the Lord, also in your thought life.
4. Ask the Lord immediately to forgive you if you sin. Also, forgive yourself and learn to love yourself.
5. Develop a lifestyle of forgiveness towards all people that you come across.
6. Make sure your relationships are in order, in as far as it depends on you (Rom.12:18).
7. Overcome that which is evil by doing what is good (Rom.12:21), asking for the help and strength of the Holy Spirit.
8. Hold on to the truth of Gods Word, whatever your feelings may tell you.
9. Count your blessings - make a list of them!
10. Do not hesitate to ask a trustworthy Christian friend for prayer and advice.

Finally, this book may also guide you in helping others. In the complicated age in which we live, where so many problems and inner wounds come up, we may lack counselors with a solid Biblical foundation. Hopefully, the advice and tips in this book, together with our prayers, may bless those around us and help them to fully place their trust in our loving heavenly Father.

1
HOW CAN WE FACE SUFFERING?

We have probably all known some suffering in our personal lives - and, sometimes, God has been blamed for it! It is then good to remember, that most of the suffering is inflicted on us by the fallen, sinful human race itself (sometimes, we even cause it ourselves) when people do not obey God and are guided by the enemy. That may not lessen our sorrow, but it does help us to find our comfort with a loving heavenly Father, who by His commandments and decrees had intended good things for us. As suffering often makes us wonder, "Who is God?" "Why does He allow it?", we will spend some extra space on such questions in this chapter.

In very difficult times in life, perhaps the following thoughts may be of help:

1.1 Walking on victory ground

We need not give room to the accuser! In difficult situations and suffering, the enemy of our souls readily comes to point with his finger to our sins and says, "It's your own fault!", or perhaps "God now punishes you". In Matth.4:3-10, the enemy even inappropriately quoted Scripture to prove his point! But Jesus replies to his suggestions with the Word of God. When we feel accused, we need to *know* that our sins have been forgiven, from the Word of God (1.Jhn.1:9; Col.1:11-14; Ac.13:38-39); it can be very helpful to learn such helpful Scriptures by heart. The certainty of forgiveness is a very important point; it is the source of our victory and the basis of our authority! Once we have been forgiven, we are walking on victory ground, even in cases where the cause of suffering *was* our own fault. Therefore, deal with your sins very carefully. We do not obtain forgiveness by fighting sins in our own strength, but by bringing these directly to the Lord Jesus and by asking Him to forgive us and to help us in our Christian walk by the strength of the Holy Spirit.

If we want to avoid sin, it is best to keep focusing on Jesus, and on all the good things He gives us to do (Rom.12:20-21; Php.4:8; Ps.16:7-11), rather than spending much time avoiding sin and thus keeping focused on that!

Often, the "little foxes" of sin spoil the vineyard of our victory (SoS.2:15), so it is important to bring your large and small sins to the Lord daily and to ask for His forgiveness - preferably, as soon as you notice these. You can do so silently, by a quiet prayer in your heart during a difficult conversation or at work. Just remain close to Him. Forgive others who caused you pain, especially those who have hurt you in the past. It is good to spend some time on that, and to ask forgiveness for your own attitude in those situations, too. Be thorough in this, and make sure you do accept the forgiveness that the Lord gives you; for then you no longer need to feel guilty and the enemy has no more room for his accusations in your life. The Lord rejoices over our upright hearts. He is a very present help in trouble (Ps.46:1-2). His love is always there for us, even though we or others have failed Him. Scripture passages such as Ps.33:16-22 and 62:1-9 may encourage you along the way.

If our hearts condemn us...

A good passage to apply is 1.John 3:19-24. We can learn how to respond when we feel guilty or under accusations. Do not immediately accept these accusations, but come to the Lord and ask Him if you have failed and where you have sinned. If He does clearly convince us that such accusations true, we know the way: we ask the Lord to forgive us, we try to put things right where possible and pray that He helps us not to do it again. Then, we can stand before the Lord as pure servants.

However, very often the accusations are *vague*, you only have a general feeling of failure. If you can find no true cause, it probably is a pure lie! Do not accept it, resist the enemy and his accusations, and thank the Lord that you are a child of the King. In case you cannot break through the sense of guilt yourself, you can ask others to pray for you; for it is of the utmost importance that we know how we can stand on victory ground, by the atonement on Calvary. Do not let go until you are secure of this - it is there for you, here and now!

When there is no reason for suffering...

Through the forgiveness of sins by our loving God we may know that the enemy can no longer point his finger at us, claiming that suffering befalls us because we stand guilty. If our sins are forgiven, we may even know that we are a new creation, in a living relationship with Christ! (2 Cor.5:17) That does not remove all suffering from our life, but we then know that it befalls us for other reasons: because other people in their sins or lack of understanding inflict it upon us, because we live in a fallen world with sickness and death in which the enemy prowls, or for Jesus' sake because we believe in Him (we are resisted by the enemy and by people who do not know God). (Php.1:28-29) However, God's grace and glory will carry us through suffering. (1.Pet.4:14; Hebr.2:9, Lk.24:26-27, Rom.8:17-18,28) Especially in suffering, He promises us His glory, and we may radiate some of it towards others. (1 Pet.2:12)

In a fallen world full of sorrow, God placed us with our own responsibility to choose for the good and to love one another. He did not make us into puppets; He allows us to make mistakes and we can even go against His will. (Mt.22:37-40) So, we are sometimes hurt by one another not because God wants this, but because He gave each of us the freedom of choice. Thus, it is possible that we sin against one another - sins for which He already developed a rescue plan, a plan that cost Jesus His own life ... He is so good!

1.2 A more abundant life

God wants to give us life more abundantly; whatever is good, acceptable, perfect (John 10:10; Rom.12:2; Ja.1:17). Abundant life - isn't that wonderful? Let this truth sink deeply into our hearts. God sent His only Son to suffer in our place and carry our guilt away. He does not want us to suffer - how could He Who spoke, "thou shalt not steal" (Ex.20:15) send us a thief? How could He Who created the ear, send us deafness? For those whose sins are forgiven, there is no more condemnation (Rom.8:1).

Many people find it hard to believe that such a good God rules over such a bad world. God has chosen to create man in such a way that he could choose for or against Gods will. What value has the love of someone who was created without an own will and who always exactly does as we would desire? With such a person, a real relationship is not possible - and God longed for a true relationship with us, one of real love in which we make a personal choice to love Him in return. Since Adam's wrong choice, sin, sickness, and death came into the world; yet by Gods Son, the Lord Jesus, victory has been won for those who love Him.

Suffering, troubles and sickness, therefore, can be tracked down to:
(a) Sins of others and/or of ourselves - God in His love wants to restore us;
(b) the world around us that has fallen into sin, resulting for instance in sickness, strife and war, etc.; and
(c) the work of Gods adversary, Satan - who is overcome by Jesus, the Son of God, through His saving work at the cross.

However, even in the suffering that still befalls us, God's plan for our lives will be worked out, as He strengthens us in the battle - and in it makes *all* things work together for good to them that love God! (Rom.8:28) God even sent His Son to suffer *in our place*; yet when our suffering comes from our own sin, or that of people around us, or by the world that has fallen into sin, or by the enemy, then those who love

Him will still bear fruit in His plan. He then lets even those situations work together for our good.

Remaining under His protection...

"But in the Bible we also read about God's punishment", some may think. Yes, that is true - and one of the ways it works is as follows. If we sin, we walk away from God like the prodigal son; we then walk beyond the protection of our heavenly Father, and the enemy can attack us. Nevertheless, even that situation is used by God to warn us and correct us and bring us back to Himself. The Good Shepherd even risks His own life to find and save us, the lost sheep. With God, punishment is not to harm us (the devil does that, to bring pain and destroy us), but a warning that we are ruining ourselves, and a correction to bring us back to the good path of restoration, healing, education, and joy.

If we want to obey the Lord Jesus with all our hearts, the Holy Spirit can guide us with the slightest push into the right direction. Yet, sometimes, God needs more radical measures to get the attention of His children when we really will not listen. It is as with a mother, who warns her child: do not touch the stove, or you'll burn your hands. If the child chooses wrongly, it withdraws from the mother's protection and burns itself painfully. Along the path of pain, it learns that this is indeed dangerous. The mother feels the pain of her child, but she knows that it needs to learn obedience and thus come within her protection. The same is true of God. God loves sinners. He is so ready to forgive; He receives us sinners with open arms, and would so much love to see us in heaven in times to come.

Jesus, the Good Shepherd, risked His own life to bring us, straying sheep, back into the safety of His sheepfold. Some of us may still be a bit sloppy in dealing with our sins (like some Christians in Hebr.12) and get entangled in the painful thorns of this sinful world. He gave us a free will to choose: to remain under His secure charge, or to stray alone and unprotected outside of the fold. Yet God even wants to use our situations of distress for our good, to bring about in us a change of heart. It is precisely the sheep that goes its own way and strays far from the Good Shepherd, that becomes entangled in the painful thorns of sin; and it is precisely *that* sheep He goes out to save at the risk of His own life. The entangled sheep suffers, calls for Him to help, and will not soon repeat its lonely venture! Therefore, it is so important that we know for sure that our sins have been brought to Him, that we have been forgiven, and that we live in safety with Him.

When we have asked for His forgiveness...

Some people believe that God punishes His people because *we* have to pay for our own mistakes. This is a misconception! The Lord Jesus has paid for our sins on the cross, *in our place*. Of course, we are to put things right with other people (if this is at all possible) and ask their forgiveness if we have done them any wrong. For we are sinners and regularly make mistakes. If we bring our sins to the Lord Jesus and embrace His forgiveness, we may know that He has borne our judgment. We can then stand with clean and open hearts before God. What a joy! (Ps.32:1-2)

But if we try to pay for our own sins (make up for mistakes by working hard for God, or by punishing ourselves and denying ourselves all sorts of things), we will - as imperfect human beings - never reach the level of this perfect God. Yet for children of God, who accept that their sins are forgiven by His grace, Jesus is the door to God (Jhn.10:1-9). He is the loving heavenly Father with Whom they find refuge. God is good, He is love, and in Him there is no darkness at all. (Ps.135:3; 145:8-9; Nah.1:7; 1.Joh.4:7-8; 1.Joh.1:5).

Warning or false accusation?

When things go wrong, we may think God does not love us anymore, or that He warns us against something - and we try to dig for some not yet forgiven sin: "There must be something wrong with me". However, not all suffering is a warning from God! Only occasionally - then it spurs us on to search our conscience for things that He wants to speak to us about. Yet when that is not the case (don't keep digging into some vague accusations, but ask for His will and His wisdom), we need to remind ourselves that the devil loves to accuse God's children. We will not accept that! *Those accusations are mostly vague* (if they were specific and true, we would immediately go to the Lord and put things right - and his bullets would be wasted). As mentioned before, this is a very important point, as many Christians are robbed of their victory in Christ by such vague feelings of guilt. Our true victory is in a conscience that has been washed clean by the blood of Jesus, forgiven and redeemed by Him (Col.1:13-14). We may then know that we are a *new creation* (2.Cor.5:7; Rom.8:1), in a living relationship with Him. The fact that we suffer may well indicate that the enemy is not happy with us as he has seen that we serve God. Yet in the midst of it all, God is our refuge and strength! (Ps.46).

Coming closer to God...

As sinners, we were born into a world fallen into sin, as in a school where we can learn to choose for whatever is good, in the midst of other sinners. *That in itself is a battle!* (Jam.1:2-3; 1.Pet.1:7; 5:6-10; 1.Jhn.5:3-5) It is not always easy to choose whatever is good, as the Bible teaches, even if we know what we should do... Yet even in the midst of this God promises us that He will help us, that He will even make all things work together for our good if we love Him (Rom.8:28-29); that we may become more like Jesus. We cannot add anything to our holiness as such, but we can learn to become more careful in bringing our sins to Jesus, to have these washed away by Him. The suffering we are in, even if this is not our fault, can make us handle these things more earnestly and carefully, and bring us closer to God. In itself, suffering does not make us holy! Suffering does not add to our salvation. Jesus Christ *suffered in our place*, at the cross. He Himself is our sanctification and redemption (1.Cor.1:30-31).

For those who serve the Lord Jesus faithfully, the suffering with which the enemy would target Gods children can be an incentive to live even closer to Jesus and seek protection and strength in His presence. God does not want us to suffer. The enemy has come to steal, kill, and destroy; but Gods Son has come to destroy the works of the devil and to bring us life, even *abundantly*! (John 10:10; 1.John 3:8) He wants to heal our hearts, and the price for the sins we brought to Him has already been paid long ago at Calvary. Sanctification is in our relationship with the living Lord by the washing away of our sins, and that remains necessary for all of us, all of our life. It is in Christ that we are sanctified; not by our good works or our suffering - therefore, it is not too hard for any of us! (1.Cor.6:10-11; 2.Cor.7:1; Hebr.10:10) Jesus Himself suffered in our place to give us *sanctification for free*, as a gift to us. We are sanctified in Him (in our living relationship with Him). Sanctification is in no one else... (Ac.4:12) We are holy "in Him", even though we may stumble again tomorrow and have to ask Him to forgive us once again. The New Testament calls such believers "saints", and we too may know that we are sanctified in Christ by the forgiveness of our sins.

Take a fresh look at God's goodness...

When we follow God obediently but have no clear view of the goodness of God yet, suffering may be very painful to us. We may then feel as if God sends us these troubles, while this suffering comes from the enemy and God wants to comfort and support us in the midst of it. If we are not sure whether our sins have been forgiven (pray to God for that certainty, it is so important!), the accuser of our souls can use this to talk us into feelings of guilt and get us convinced that our situation is hopeless: "things will never work out for you anyway". Thank God that that is *not* true! With God, there is *always* new hope and redemption, again and again, whatever the situation may be. An important part of our spiritual battle lies in knowing this. God wages our battles for us, He is on *our* side. He does not forget us (Ps.27), and right in the midst of those hard situations His eye is upon us; He desires to encourage and comfort us. The picture of a hard, inaccessible God is a wrong image that the enemy tries to hold before us. Do not fall into that trap, for God *is* love (1.John 4:1-12). What God in fact has intended for us can be seen in the original situation: paradise, and in the final goal: heaven.

1.3 Being comforted by God

God can work in many ways to comfort our hearts:

A. We can read in the Scriptures (Rom.15:4) how others were comforted and encouraged in hardships, how they received a deepening of their faith and an anointing from God. The Psalms have much to say on this, especially those by David (who knew much suffering in his own life). Just read in Ps. 16, 18, 23, 25, 27, 31, 34, 42-43, 46, 55, 62, 71, 86, 91, 119, etc. The same is true for Scriptures like Is.40-45, Mt.5, John 14, or letters like those to the Ephesians, Philippians, Colossians, and the first letter of Peter. In reading these, God can speak to us personally, and His Word always brings light and life. Reach out to Him, therefore, listening intently to Him, to His word for your specific situation. Also, the Bible gives many practical tips on what to do in difficult circumstances: Mt.5:4, 10:19,288-31; 26:41; John 2:6a; 17:22-23; Ro.5:3-5; 8:14-39; 12:12-21; 1.Cor.4:9-13; 2.Cor.4:7-18; 12:9-10; Eph.6:10-19; Php.1:27-2:16; Col.4:5-6; 1.Thess.5:15-18; 2.Tim.2:3-4; 4:5; Heb.11:24-27; Rev.2:10; and so many others.

B. *Often, we can be comforted and encouraged by those around us.* We may often have been touched by the spiritual depth in some peoples' lives (not only in the Bible, but also of those around us), who have known much suffering without getting bitter. One could divide the Christian flock in two categories: *the diamonds and the pearls*. The diamond is strong and hard; the impurities and rough spots have to be scoured and polished away for it to sparkle clearly or for its strength to be used. A pearl, however, is not strong but starts as a little grain of sand within the oyster. Because it hurts, the oyster covers it with a beautiful layer to become a pearl. However, both in the diamond and the oyster, after the pain the beautiful colors of God's rainbow can be seen! No matter to which category of sufferers you belong, God is turning your life into something beautiful. Many precious stones are mentioned in the Bible, and it can be surprising, for instance, to look up Scriptures on the "pearl" in a concordance. One day, in the new Jerusalem, the gates will each be made of a single pearl. The pearl is, so to speak, a picture of the openness that sensitive people have received for others through their suffering.

C. *We can be comforted by remembering God's love.* As we sit at His feet, finding refuge with Him, we can enjoy His presence and learn from Him. In those moments, He can give us His rest and fragrance. We need these precious moments, especially in times of hardship, where we can pour out our hearts to Him and be comforted.

Moreover, it can be quite helpful to write down in a special notebook, which *answers to prayer, comforting words and promises* the Lord has already given you in the past, especially from his Word. Look for what encourages you and brings hope in your present situation. Treasure these things as precious jewels, remember to write them down in the notebook, and keep it at hand! Sometimes, when we feel despondent, we may think: Has God really seen me? Does He know, does He care? At such times, it helps to remember the times when He did speak to us in the past, and when He blessed us. If we review such special blessings and real answers from our notebook, this will encourage us when life seems especially hard. You may add the date and situation when God spoke, like a *"Book of Remembrance"* (Mal.3:16). If you have never done so before, you may start writing today - adding whatever you can remember from what He has done in your life from the start. Such a notebook can be a tremendous help and comfort in times when God seems far away; it will build up your faith, and as you go back in it, you may be able to see a larger picture develop through the years. In certain busy times, I failed to keep track of God's blessings, and have been very sorry later! So: do store your gems...

D. *Finally, we can be comforted by the experiences of others.* It can be of much help to *read good books* that build up your character and encourage you, for instance about people who through times of difficulty and weakness were used by God (such as stories of missionaries) or books that relate to the situation that you are presently in.

1.4 Pray for a new revelation of the Lord

In the numerous questions that come to us in times of suffering, it can be truly refreshing to receive a new awareness of God's loving presence, His tender touch by the Holy Spirit, a Scripture verse in which God speaks to us very personally, or a prophetic message to help us see the path ahead. God will certainly hear our prayer when our heart truly reaches out for Him. We may not yet know why all these things happen to us, but we know that

Jesus' eye is upon us - He understands us, He knows and accepts us. His tender look of interest gives us such encouragement and new strength. Do we have the courage to put our trembling hands into His?

Our certainty lies not in the circumstances, even though the Lord would like to take part and help us in those, but our certainty is in Him Who is the answer to all our questions. It is so comforting and healing to know, that He - the "I AM" - is with us, that He guides us, even though we may not yet see the next step ahead. This is not just about a mental knowledge of God and His character, but about a revelation of who God is in our own life, and finding the way to His almighty presence. It is not only that God will let all things work together for our good (Rom.8:28) or that what He arranges for us here on earth will make the burden of our suffering lighter; it is His presence itself (John 16:33). However great and mighty He is, He is always there for us. That deep awareness of His presence is enough, and it gives a new perspective and depth and meaning to life. He truly knows and accepts us; that opens us up and gives us confidence in the midst of the perhaps turbulent events around us.

Our suffering can be so deep, that nothing else will help us but a renewed personal meeting with the Almighty God. It is so good to spend much time with Him (Php.3:7-11).

1.5 Invite Jesus into your sorrow

The Lord Jesus suffered in our place, for our sins, out of His own free will - because He loved us. He was not welcome when He came into the world; He had to be born in a stable. Our heart often looks like that poor and perhaps dirty stable; and yet we may know that He comes in gladly (Rev.3:20; Jhn.6:37-40; 7:37). How much would we have preferred to welcome Him into a beautiful home... However, He has been used to stables since His earliest childhood; and He is the only one who can truly clear up the mess in the stable of our heart. We cannot pay Him to do that for us. He paid for it Himself with His own life.

Therefore, we do not need to fear that He might see what things really look like inside. Wouldn't we invite Him in then? He is so eager to come!

So, we do invite Him in. First, we feel a bit uneasy - would He really come into our battered and torn heart? He has seen it all and wants to forgive: for He accepts the invitation. As we begin to understand what His forgiveness means, we start to relax a bit. He comes and sits with us - His eyes are friendly, as though they seek real contact. It is very quiet for a while. We start sitting more comfortably in our chairs, take courage and look at Him, and into His eyes... and then it hits us: He is a Man of Sorrows. With eyes that have already seen everything - all the sorrow of this world, that He carried for you and me. If, in the midst of all pain, you have dared look into those eyes, then you know you are understood and accepted unto the very depths of your being. We start feeling at home with this Friend that we can trust in our sadness. His presence works out healing and peace. Even at this moment, He stands with open arms towards us. He longs to be born into the stable of our heart and to carry our loads.

Isn't it amazing that there is fullness of joy in the presence of the Man of Sorrows? (Ps. 16; 2.Cor.6:10). With Him, we can be sorrowful yet always rejoicing. Let us take much time to sit with Jesus, right in the rooms of our hearts where the sorrows are hidden, and give our pain to Him. Put your sorrow and difficulties into His pierced hands. He truly understands; and in that, He is a reflection of our loving heavenly Father.

If your goals are unattainable, if your dreams are gone, remember that in essence He is your dream and your goal - and He has not changed! He who took all our guilt upon Himself also wants to comfort us in the pain of our lost earthly ideals. His promises still stand; there is always new hope with Him.

In the Bible, there are so many beautiful verses on "hope" that it would be impossible to mention all of them here! (It's worth looking them up in a concordance.)

1.6 Do not push your sorrow down, but face it

These days it is not the "in" thing to show your sadness. The world already knows so much sadness that it wants to laugh it away. Even among Christians, we like to radiate victory, security, and joy. You soon push your sorrow away, fearing to be seen as less popular, less strong; or perhaps you feel you have misunderstood God's will for your life.

However, suffering does not necessarily mean that we have been disobedient. Remember that Jesus, our obedient and guiltless Savior, still suffered like no one else - because He loved us. He was more courageous than any of us, and yet He was sad and wept, even though He always was in the center of God's will! (Mt.26:37-39; Lk.19:41; John 11:33-35). God Himself will often be sad when He looks at this world, and He suffers with us when we are sad. We too may shed tears before the Lord if that relieves us. Yet if crying does not relieve us but makes us even more depressed, we need to decide to consciously stop it and start looking upon Jesus! Otherwise, there is a chance that we hand ourselves over to negative feelings that do not come from our God of hope; and we need to especially avoid all self-pity (see also in Chapter 2). With God, there are always new possibilities. Knowing God, our contact with Him, cheers us up and brings peace, even in the midst of difficulties. That makes the joy we find with Him so very special, like a refreshing oasis in the desert.

Therefore, allow yourself to deal with sorrow by facing the facts together with the Lord. With Him, there is no need for self-pity or for judging yourself harshly, nor for disappointment or even bitterness - Jesus never harbored those, so neither will we (we may *choose* against it, again and again). But we can face the sorrow together with Jesus - a real sadness, a "godly sorrow" (2.Cor.7:9-11) that grieves for the things God also grieves about and in which we may know that He feels with us and stands next to us. That can be when we have had to miss a loved one, when there is an operation or difficult circumstances, when someone hurts us or sins against us, if we have sinned ourselves and are sorry for it; or if we are persecuted for Jesus' sake.

So, do not run away from your own feelings, but let the Lord enter into the "sorrow-room" of your heart. He knows about sorrows, He is no Stranger there... He helps us to forgive those causing us sorrow and to pray for them as long as God brings that burden to our heart. We may bring the situation before Gods throne, as often as we think about it, and slowly it will lose its sting - and forgiveness gets rooted deeply within us.

We can also practically deal with a painful situation. I know of a couple that lost a young child. They have put together a scrap-book with all the precious photographs and souvenirs of their child, and thus came to terms with their sorrow - not by running away from the pain but by constructively dealing with it, and by letting the Lord take part in their sorrow. You can also tell other people which you trust about your sorrow once you feel you are able to do that. Their listening ear, their prayers and friendship will encourage and help us. We need not be ashamed of our sorrows.

1.7 Tapping into the great fountain of joy

We come close to the source of joy by frequently coming into the quiet presence of the Lord Jesus, who sends us the

Holy Spirit, the Comforter. (John 15:26) However difficult the circumstances are, the Holy Spirit who wants to live in us more and more, will work out within us His fruit of love, joy, peace, etc. (Gal.5:22-23) We cannot grow this fruit ourselves, but God wants to reveal Himself in our life by it. Therefore, just open up yourself frequently to the infilling with the Holy Spirit, and ask Him often to enter with His joy. That way, we learn to tap God's fountain of joy and to expect Him to work.

Joy is also something we can *choose*. We can choose to remember the good things around us, of which there are always some, and to thank God often for them. That way, whatever is good and beautiful becomes established in our heart. As we direct ourselves more towards whatever is lovely and pure, and "count our blessings", our painful soul can more easily be lifted up and healed. So often, the Bible calls on us to be thankful whatever the circumstances, and to rejoice in the Lord. (Php.4:4-8) Therefore, this is a divine commission. Learning to follow that order needs practice, and a choice to work on this with God's help - but with what blessed results!

Finally, there is *heaven*, in which we can rejoice every day. Not too long ago, I felt as if God pointed this out to me. At first, my response wasn't very enthusiastic: "Lord, I do not want to die yet!" Of course, that was not really what He had meant, and when I wanted to obey I discovered that I had put my whole life into His hands, but not the moment of my death... Only after I gave that moment to Him - not without battle - I can indeed look forward to heaven. The problems on earth will increase, but we can direct our thoughts toward our most precious inheritance: heaven, where we will receive an unspeakable joy. (Luk.21:25-28; 1.Pet.1:3-11; Rom.8:17-19; 1.Cor.2:9; Rev.7:14-17).

1.8 A special opportunity to honor Jesus

In suffering, we find a very special opportunity to bring joy to the heart of Jesus, because we then no longer serve Him for what we receive from Him in return, but give a sacrifice of praise, for who He is! It is, perhaps, the *only* thing *we* can really give to Him: as in the midst of suffering we do love, honor and obey Him without complaint. That is a chance we may really use - and our life thus becomes a sacrifice of praise! A real sacrifice is never given without effort. The Lord says: He who offers thanksgiving as his sacrifice glorifies Me. (Ps.50:23) Moreover, God will give us His Holy Spirit when we suffer for His sake (1.Pet.4:12-14).

We do not need to keep focusing on our feelings, but can look up to Him as our loving Savior and Redeemer who understands and loves us. Right in the midst of our sadness, He sits with us. We are safe with Him. He remains faithful - and as we realize this, our feelings of pain will receive less and less space and influence in our life. Try to thank and glorify God for all the good things that He has given, especially when the world fails us. Thoughts of sadness need not become a pattern in this situation, and it is good to use this opportunity to bring joy to His heart in a special way - for He knows our love for Him does not come lightly. We bring joy to the heart of God if we love Him and sing to Him, even if our feelings cannot keep up.

1.9 In times of suffering our spiritual life deepens

A. Renewed prayer life

Difficult times bring us closer to the Lord Jesus and make us seek times of quietness, to speak to Him and be comforted by Him. As we seek His face more often, our prayer life will deepen. Our dedication to Him can find renewal there, and our obedience can increase. (2.Chron.16:9; Php.3:9-10; 2.Thess.3:3-5; Is.40:29-31)

B. Renewed strength

Furthermore, this can be a time that strengthens our character as we go into battle, like David who had to suffer so much. (Ps.144:1-2; Ps.18:30-36) As we try to deepen the living relationship with the Lord Jesus, we find that He is the source of our strength. Thus, through times of battle and of quietness before Him, God can give us a new cleansing, empowering, and authority for our task. For in times of difficulty we learn to trust Him, and also to encourage and comfort others through the lessons of life that we experienced ourselves. In such times we also notice that our spiritual life becomes deeper and purer, and that through it God can touch our wounds and weaknesses at a deeper level than normal. Now that they surface, He can work on them. Sometimes, fasting for a day or two in a quiet place can strengthen us in such times, while we take time to ask God for more insight into our situation. Perhaps some lies of the enemy harm us and need to be replaced by the truth. We can be encouraged by beautiful Scriptures on this. (Rom.16:20; 1.Pet.2:12; 3:13-16; 4:4; 2.Tim.3:12; 4:5).

C. Deeper security

A time of set-back or problems will also show us if our security is in the Lord, or in our circumstances, our possessions, friends, etc. - even our petty "idols" that compete with the Lord and that He wants to deal with. Only very strong legs can carry the wealth of never-ending success, riches, and wonderful circumstances. Problems help us to see things in more realistic proportions, and in our inadequacy drive us towards the Lord. God uses such times to let us grow more quickly spiritually than would otherwise be possible, and thus we can come to inner maturity. In adverse circumstances, we learn to seek and find the truth. We learn to lean on Jesus, who says, "I am the truth" and "the truth will set you free". (John 14:6; 8:32-36)

D. Deeper obedience

We can exercise ourselves in obedience. In times of sorrow and difficulties, in which the enemy could lead us away from obedience more easily, we find an opportunity to exercise our spiritual muscles by remaining faithful and obedient, also in small matters. It is written of Jesus, that He learned obedience from the things He suffered. (Heb.5:8) If life goes smoothly for us, it is not so hard to really obey; yet if there is a price tag to it, when obedience may even increase our suffering, it develops our character and we grow closer to Jesus. Thus, it is a time when we learn how to pray and to find our refuge in God. (Jam.5:13; Prov.18:10)

E. Deeper forgiveness

Such times of deep lessons also concern our relationships: especially now it is a challenge to love difficult people (also compare Ch.8) and to forgive others completely. (Mt.5:44) It is also much easier to understand God's voice for our situation if our conscience is clear, and if we have restored our relationships (in as far as it depends on us). (Rom.12:18; Hebr.12:14) Especially now, it is a challenge to be a blessing for others, and to bring some of our weaknesses to Jesus that would hardly surface when all goes well... (1.Thess.5:23-24)

F. A fruitful time

The situation we find ourselves in may continue for some time, but its opportunities may never be duplicated. Therefore, let us decide to fully use this chance to let Him mould our character more into His image, even if the times are painful (Rom.8:29; 2.Cor.3:18; Col.3:10). In all these things, He is very close to us; His anointing often comes in the valley periods of our lives, where light does not fully penetrate, and where we learn to really trust Him. The streams of living water flow to the lowliest spots! The author C.S. Lewis appears to have said, that in every stumbling block a calling lies hidden. God wastes not even our hardships, but uses them. (Rom.8:28)

Therefore, we can reap a harvest from this time; a time in which we can be filled with the Holy Spirit, and grow closer to the Lord and to others; a time to lean more on God than on people and circumstances, to become spiritually mature, and also to learn spiritual warfare. Through these experiences we can learn true compassion for others instead of just pity - weeping with those who weep (Rom.12:15). That, too, is one of the abiding fruits in our life through such periods: real sensitivity and compassion towards others may especially be found in the lives of those who have suffered themselves and who in it were prepared by God for tasks like pastoral work or evangelism.

1.10 Learning how to comfort others

Out of the lessons God has taught us throughout our own difficulties, we can learn how to comfort others - as we show concern about their sorrows and focus on making people around us happy. (Prov.12:25; 2.Cor.1:3-7; 1.Cor.12:26; Rom.12:15; Eccl.7:2) Ask the Lord how you may best encourage them - by a truth that He lays within your heart, a Scripture verse, or simply by some flowers, a cake or practical help. Even our listening ear in itself can be an encouragement to them. We will better recognize their moods if we know these from our own experience! If we have learned not to hide our own sorrows, we will feel less uncomfortable at their tears, and will handle the situation more naturally.

Make sure not to leave others when they are not behaving like the popular crowd. In their sorrow, they may perhaps draw back. Let's not push ourselves on them, but wait quietly and prayerfully for an opportunity to briefly visit and speak to them. Moreover, we need not ask them any questions if we are not sure they are willing to answer; yet being very sensitive towards them. They may remain quiet with true friends. We do not always need to say much; but we can stand with them in openness, and let them know that we appreciate them.

A brief visit or picture postcard, even with a few words only, can let them know that they are in our thoughts (if we really know nothing to write, we can put "Wishing you much strength" or "May God bless you richly", and our name). Especially, let us not forget to pray for them; it is one of the best things we can do for them.

Moreover, we can remember things that have strengthened and comforted us when we were sorrowful ourselves, so that we can do the same thing for them (2.Cor.1:4). We can then do it in a more natural way because it spoke to our own heart, and because we experienced that it works! This is also true for practical situations. For instance, we may invite them for a walk or some other relaxing activity, in which they can come to another mindset without needing to give all their attention to other people or to talking. Some people can be helped if we ask for their practical assistance in a real need in our own life, so that their mind is directed to other things than their problems without needing to talk much. Others can be helped by our listening ear and time, when they need to talk things over.

We can learn to listen to those in sorrow, and when they have fully finished their own talking - if they are open to it - we may tell them of our own battles and what we have learned - if we can do so without interrupting or putting new burdens on them! Pray that we may help them to not run away from their own feelings but to face their situation, by showing true interest. We can encourage them and remain faithful to them. Be a true friend. Learning to comfort others is also a real comfort to ourselves!

2
WHEN WE FEEL DOWN-HEARTED OR DEPRESSED

Life has its ups and its downs for each of us, although sometimes it seems the downs take the upper hand! We may then feel sad, discouraged, and gloomy. However, just as the water of the life-bringing river gathers in the valley, so the Holy Spirit wants to especially fill these low areas in our lives to encourage and refresh us in a time of need, and to accomplish a deep work within us (Ps.23) where otherwise we might not take the time to open ourselves up to Him. That way, He wants to give us new strength - for such times are often times of battle. He also wants to comfort us, for in the valley the view is limited. However, the deeper the valley, the higher the mountains and the greater the view!

When we are in the valley anyway, it is important to *lean on God* - something we can learn in practice by seeking His face. Thus, we may even draw profit from this time and situation, by asking God to help us and work in us more deeply, as we wrestle with Him through problems and questions, and thus become stronger.

The following thoughts are intended to help us make room in our heart for Gods presence and healing.

2.1 Reading about the goodness of God in the Bible

Much has been written about the goodness of God, especially in the Psalms, and the more we become aware of His goodness whatever our circumstances, the less grip the enemy will have on us. Therefore, it is very important to understand God's character correctly, He who loved us so much that His only Son died for us! (Jn.3:16) We may not *feel*

His goodness in our emotions, but we can purposely *soak* our spirit with the truth of God's intense goodness towards us (see also Ch.5.3), knowing that this is the truth God's Word states. It is great to know that - even though our feelings may be wounded and therefore unreliable - the truth of God's faithfulness and love for us will always stand.

How do we get rid of our negative thoughts, even about the character of God? By being aware of them, and by asking Him to forgive us that we did let them in. We learn from the Bible that God is truly good, a loving heavenly Father, and our mind can speak this to our weary soul (Ps. 42:11). It will also help us to keep thanking Him that He is love, and that He will be victorious in our life. Thus, we will not be an actor or a pretender, for these statements are based on the *facts*! In His enormous power, He even won the victory over death and hell; how much more can He then be victorious in us, small people, whom He loves so intensely.

A favorite lie of the enemy is: "There is no hope left for you". This type of insinuation is a clear sign of his work, and we need not tolerate this in our thinking any longer! This statement is never the truth, *never*. Gods salvation is for everyone (!) who comes to Him; with Him there is always new hope (Jn.6:7; Mt.11:28-29; Gal.2:20-21; Rom.15:13). If sometimes thoughts of doubt keep harassing us, and if then in prayer to God we cannot shake these thoughts off, it is right for us to ask others who have more experience in these things to pray for us - for instance, a trusted church leader.

Neither do we need to fight our unbelief in our own strength, but we can confess it, ask for God's forgiveness and accept it, and decide to take only the Bible as the truth. To be happy, your heart may understand (and say this out loud regularly) that God is pleased with you, that He values you, that He stands next to you when you fall, that He has forgiven all sin and guilt that you have brought before Him, and that He leads and carries you in the midst of all difficulties. His character is one of hope and mercy; of love, joy, peace, patience, kindness, goodness, faithfulness, gentleness and self-control (Gal.5:22-23) - all the things that

He wants to develop in us, too. Jesus Himself is our wisdom, righteousness, sanctification and redemption (1.Cor.1:30), and it is wonderful that we are "in Him"!

2.2 Sit at Jesus' feet frequently

In Jesus' presence, we find rest. He Himself has suffered so much and understands us like no one else. A yoke that oppresses us and breaks us down does not come from Him Who loves us (Mt.11:28-30; Jer.29:11-13). In such a situation, we may ask for His wisdom, and what He wants us to carry for Him and for His name's sake, so that He can be glorified through us. In the silence, very close to Him, we experience His guidance, safety, sweet tenderness and joy; there is the fresh fountain that we can draw from (1.Sam.30:6B; Ps.16:7-11; 21:1). There, too, our feelings come to rest, and we start seeing things more clearly.

If Jesus is our *"first love"* (Rev.2:4), nothing will be able to overcome us. He is our comfort and our strength. Difficulties may sometimes test our love, but they will only make it stronger when we make this "first love" our goal. Then, we also start realizing that His love for us is unconditional and that it does not depend on our achievements (Rom.4:5; 5:6-9; 1.Jn.4:9-10). For some of us, this is a difficult lesson, as we may often feel we should make ourselves worthy of His love, and that we must earn it. However, Jesus, our best Friend, is always there for us! With Him, we can freely show our feelings. Our life is unbelievably precious in His sight. The prayer of the smallest, most disappointed, dejected or rejected Christian is still of great importance to Him. Even if we can no longer pray, He rejoices in us and boundlessly loves us; He is always ready to listen and forgive, to encourage and comfort. Know the love of the Lord! He is such a great Comforter (2.Thess.2:16-17).

2.3 A way to "pray without ceasing" (1.Thess.5:17)

We can pray throughout the day, with open eyes: during a walk, while sitting on a bike, and even during a conversation (the others do not need to notice that you are speaking to God in your heart). Thus, we can bring all our burdens to the Lord continually. Also, it helps to remember the possibility of praying in the Holy Spirit, to be built up by Him! (Jude 20; Eph.6:18; Rom.8:26-27) He prays through and for us if we ourselves can no longer find the words. Through the Holy Spirit, we will find strength in our situation when we can no longer find it ourselves. Let us give Him much room in our life.

Therefore, it helps to always pray for the infilling of the Holy Spirit, as He is the perfect Comforter and Helper (Jn.14:16-17). Especially in times of suffering, when we enter into silence more often to seek the Lord, we can receive a new anointing from Him for the task that lies ahead. Perhaps now we need more of the anointing by the Holy Spirit and more awareness of the presence of the Lord for the increasing challenges that come across our path. God can then use such situations to bring us closer to Himself, and to bring us to a new level of faith and vision, where - even though we realize our own weakness - we have begun to see more of His love and presence. Therefore, let's ask the Lord regularly to permeate us with the awareness of His presence, His love, and especially His power in our daily situations. (Ac.1:8; Eph.3:20). We can then better handle the difficulties in our own life and that of others. Moreover, the Holy Spirit also wants to bring us His joy! (Ac.13:52; Rom.15:13; Gal.5:22-23; Eph.5:18-20).

2.4 Spending time in worship

In worship lies a tremendous power. It brings much joy to the heart of God when we give Him our praise, especially when that costs us something. For then, we give unselfishly. Praise during hardships is one of the few things that we can give unselfishly to Him! With our songs of worship and the glory we give to Him, we keep confirming with our mouth, while also speaking to our soul, how loving and good God is. At the same time, in worship we meet with Him. The Holy Spirit, the Comforter, can then work within our life and give us His strength. Our feelings often let us down, so that we have to *choose* to worship Him, and firmly decide to hold on to the truth of God's love and goodness without letting the enemy take this truth away from us. In worship, we concentrate on God's glory, and not on the suffering in the world that without Him we could not handle. Hebrews 1:1-4 and 12:2 give us such a beautiful example of that! A great joy lies before us. By our praise we will delight the heart of God and, especially when this is a sacrifice for us, we ourselves will be blessed as well (Ps.50:23).

Worship is honoring and thanking God for who He is, in spite of our circumstances. We can, for instance, set time aside for Him to seek His presence and to sing. If you do not find that easy, it may help you to join a church choir. Sometimes, if things make it too hard for you to sing, you can also play a tape with beautiful worship songs.

2.5 Count your blessings...

Learn, as stated in 1.Thess.5:18, to thank God *in* whatever happens (not *for* all these things, for some of these may not be according to His will - for instance, if a thief steals your purse). Do not rely on your feelings in thanking God, but decide that you will do it. If we wait until *all* circumstances are favorable, the time will never be right - perhaps we will even blame God for any harm that the devil or people have caused (God has not stolen your purse, He has even clearly warned all men against stealing). Philippians 4:6 gives tremendous advice!

Once in a while, we can choose our own "day of blessings" (or, perhaps, a "morning of blessings") and spend the time singing to the Lord, while counting our blessings and thanking Him for whatever good and positive things we can find, even when there are problems around us. Our hope is in the Lord, not in our moods and feelings. A walk in the woods can be a great opportunity to worship and thank Him. Such a day can be like a refreshing shower that gives us a better outlook and deepens our relationship with the Lord.

It can also be a good idea to start a "Notebook of thanksgiving", in which we write down everything for which we can thank God, for His promises and consolations in our life, and for the beautiful things in the past and the present. To these, we can add funny events, joyful memories, compliments or good notes we received, nice vacations, and things that bring a smile to our face. In my life, for instance, such an event is an African student in the Netherlands, who witnessed snow for the first time. Whenever I remember his happy surprise, the throwing of snowballs, and his very wide grin of excitement, it brings a smile to my face!

Such a notebook will help us to look out for the good things and in difficult times thank God, and it will lift our heart. It may also help you to ask for God's help at the beginning of the day, and to add any positive things of that day to the notebook. Then, when you feel low, you can read the list through! That way, we also learn to trust God in His goodness. I once read, that gratitude shows the measure of our spiritual maturity...

2.6 Realize who you are, through your relationship with Jesus

Many have not yet discovered, what a great gift it is to be "in Christ". If our sins have been forgiven, and if we also bring new sins to Christ immediately, then the enemy has no legal ground left to accuse us of these (even if he may try). Therefore, it is important that we know that our sins have been forgiven, that we are *a new creation in Christ* (2.Cor.5:17) and that we may consider ourselves "dead unto sin yet alive unto God" in our living relationship with Jesus Christ (Rom.6:11). We are now children of God, with all pertaining rights, and created to be kings and priests! (Rev.1:6) The Father accepts us in Christ; more than that - in Him we are *loved*. If that were not enough: He Himself has designed a plan especially for our life, that it may glorify Him. He does this, in full knowledge of our weaknesses - He has counted that in - so that we may truly know that we can walk His way as we hold onto His hand. God has been able to do some very special things through people who thought that they had totally failed Him, like Peter who had denied Jesus three times, and Paul who had persecuted the church.

Therefore, accept yourself ... and the grace of God, His loving opinion about you. Thank the Lord that He wants to use you as you are. You may be old, ugly, slow, unpopular (fill in your own imperfections), but He can use *you* for His glory. Even all these things will work together for good to those who love God (Rom.8:18). The life of many suffering Christians is an example of this. Thank the Lord that He created you for His wonderful purpose. The weaker you are, the more God can show others that it is His grace working through you. God accepts you as you are, He holds on to you even if you can no longer hold on to yourself - in times when you can no longer accept yourself or when you lack faith. God still believes in you! He knows whom He has created. He knows both your weakness and your potential strength "in Christ"! (Php.4:13) He even especially loves us when we are feeling down or have problems. We need to do *nothing* to be accepted by God, and may simply accept what Jesus has already done for us at the cross, in our place. So we freely bring to Him all our sins and weakness, to receive forgiveness and the full riches of His grace.

The heavenly Father has such loving thoughts about you - you are precious to Him, unique in the world, and He appreciates what He created in you. By accepting His loving opinion about us, we will receive a new outlook. Therefore, whenever we find ourselves doubting or rejecting who we are, it will help us to immediately ask for His forgiveness for such thoughts, and to remember what His truth is about us. Look for these truths in God's Word! Scriptures like Ps.16:8,11; Is.43:1,4; 54:4; Rom.8:31-39; Col.1:13-14; 3:1-3; or Matth.11:29-30, are good to learn by heart in case later on we fall again into the old negative pattern of introspection.

2.7 God has a goal for our life (Rom.12:2; Jer.29:11-14)

Do not forget in the valley what God has shown you previously when you were on the mountaintop. If, like so many people, we do not yet know what the true calling of our life is, we may ask the Lord to show us more of it - and to also tell us how we can become a light in the present darkness. We wait quietly and prayerfully for His guidance; it mostly unfolds step by step. Then, we will not keep focusing on the past, but can direct our eyes and hope towards the Lord Jesus and the future that He has prepared for us. Ask Him for guidance, also about how to handle the present situation constructively, as a *short-term goal*. By doing that, we do not live "out of the problem situation" (which basically is only a small part of our life), but out of the realm of all that which is good, acceptable and perfect - which is God's true goal and will for us all (Rom.12:2) - and of which He wants to show us something even now. We can always look forward to meeting with Him; we can receive more of His vision by focusing on His love, and by occupying our thoughts with all that He has for us. His Word is such a treasure chamber!

It will also help us to remember that this hard stage in our life will come to an end, and that new things will come up on the horizon. Difficult situations may prove to be a one-time chance to teach us valuable lessons. Things that now may seem insurmountable to us will in due time change or fade into the background. But as long as the situation persists, God will give us strength in the battle. We can only truly learn His precious lessons by practicing them in real life. Together with the temptation, He has also promised to provide a way of escape (1.Cor.10:13; 2.Pet.2:9). Therefore, especially now is a time to open up to His guidance and to pray for what He wants to develop within us - and, often, this is related to the future task that He prepares us for. That may not make "today" any easier, but it does give us a better perspective! We can then even use the situation, now that we are in it, to train ourselves in battle (Ps.144:1-2; 2.Cor.10:3-5; Eph.6:10-13) and to deepen our relationship with God through it. Thus, we can see that even our weakness can play a part in the goal and plan of God for our life, and that He wants to use it for our good.

I once noticed how this worked through the life of a well-known Bible teacher, by whom I had the privilege of being taught. He was a man who had quite a problem with stammering in his lectures, so he only said things that were to the point and worthy of his efforts - in as few words as possible. This saintly man was also a well-known author, and there his "battle for words" came in so well! His books were not only of high value, but very well and concisely written. His example of dedication and persistence has encouraged and inspired me.

If our own happiness is our goal, we may not know any lasting peace; if knowing God and gladdening His heart is our goal, we will receive His gladness as a by-product, while our old self dies the fastest death! May it be our highest wish that Jesus is glorified through our life, that we get to know Him more intimately. Then others may start reading in us a "letter from Christ". From getting to know Him more deeply, we grow in wisdom and vision and can start sharing with others, instead of just receiving. To those who start sowing, He has promised a harvest! (Ps.126:5-6; Gal.6:9)

2.8 Finding the cause of despondent and gloomy feelings

We can try to remember when such feelings happened in the past, and during what kind of occasions they started. What triggered your feelings this time? There mostly is a cause! It can be necessary to really spend time on trying to find this out. Make sure that you have forgiven everyone who caused you such feelings (especially also those from the past) in your heart, and then bring those situations to the Lord Jesus. He understands. He can help us to truly forgive (instead of pushing nasty memories away). We may also ask the Lord's forgiveness for our own negative attitude in some of these situations. Forgive yourself, too. That way, the enemy has no foothold in your life. Your heart can open up to others and receive healing; also, your insight into your own response to circumstances will increase.

Some of the causes for our feelings of gloom or despondency can be:

A. *Feelings of guilt - be it in small matters or in larger ones.* We can find rest as we confess our sins, and everything else that weighs heavily on our hearts, to God in Jesus' Name. We may then consciously accept forgiveness. Should, even after forgiving and having received forgiveness, the burden on our heart not have diminished, then it is quite possible that such a burden does not come from God. We may resist it! Don't give such old accusations any room whatsoever (1.Pet.5:6-9; Eph.4:27; 6:10-18). Once God has forgiven us a sin, it *is* forgiven. The enemy hates it if we realize this, and often keeps his accusations vague. It is fine with him if we keep harboring old feelings of guilt or the negative emotions that result from them. Withstand him in the name of Jesus, whenever he accuses us again of the old sins that we have already asked God's forgiveness for. Persist in standing on the forgiveness of sins that you have already brought to Jesus, and direct yourself to praising the loving heavenly Father Who made you a "new creation" through the forgiveness of your sins (2.Cor.5:17-18). Often, we are not used to thinking of ourselves in this way, but we may convince ourselves of the fact that it has been written in God's Word! We may realize our forgiven state more and more when we start thanking God for it, and enjoy the truth of being a "new creation".

B. *A difficult event, such as death in the family, divorce, or loss of a job.* These are very real difficulties that we cannot change, and we do well to seek help (if necessary, medical help) if we cannot overcome our gloomy feelings. Others can pray for us, too, and stand next to us. In such times we can experience the tremendous strength we draw from our faith and from Christian fellowship. However low you feel, try to remain involved there!

C. *Feelings of deep loneliness* (more on this can be found in Chapter 7). Here, it also helps not to feel sorry for ourselves, but to try and help others in similar situations. We cannot force others to love us, but *we* can decide to love others, and can ask God to help us find the friends that He has for us.

D. *Facing a difficult situation, where there is seemingly no way out.* Of course, we will do all to resolve the situation we are in. We may face a very difficult situation at home or at work. If that situation is there to stay, for instance if we can find no other job, there are a few things we can hold on to. Firstly, it can help us to remain close to the Lord and His Word, and to just face one day at a time. God gives strength for each step at a time, and we may hold on to Him as He guides us in relationships, finances, and all that we find difficult. Secondly, the Body of Christ can be a tremendous source of help and strength to us, as we visit Bible studies where we can be encouraged by fellow-Christians and ask for their prayers. Moreover, it helps to find a "fixed time of rest" for ourselves every week, to relax and read a good book, to go swimming or to visit a trusted friend. Be faithful to yourself in this, as you need to unwind from the extra strain and stress of daily life. Being too busy keeps the stress and makes us less able to cope with difficult situations and heavy demands. We need to remind ourselves, that there are at least *some* nice things in life! Those things can be there every week, if we let them.

E. *Unresolved hidden anger*. Let's not be too quick to say that we are not angry. For a long time, I believed I had no anger. Until I realized I had tucked it away as being the "unchristian response" that seemed unlawful! Yes, the Bible says that we are to put away all anger and bitterness (Col.3:8-13). And yes, we are to love our enemies (Mt.5:44). However, it can be a mighty release to have a good look at our anger and resolve it! How can we ask God to forgive us if we deny our anger? We often need God's help to even find our anger. Are there any people who wronged or harmed you, who were unkind to you, and in your heart those thoughts keep coming back, even though perhaps you keep forgiving them? Some of it may be unrighteous anger - that person took the job I had wanted, etc. Our response is not to like that person, and we hide it all. Why not face it? Only then can we ask God to forgive us and to restore the relationship with that person. Perhaps God gave him or her that task...

However, some of our anger may be truly righteous, and if we hide that righteous anger, we hurt both ourselves and the other person. Here, we need much love and wisdom from the Lord. If we disagree with an unfair statement or sinful action by someone else, we may truly be angry - if only we speak it out (see also Ch.8(9)). They have a right to know! This can best be done in private; Matth.18:15-17 has some very important things to say on that... Also, the Bible tells us to "not let the sun go down on our anger" (Eph.4:26-32) - so we had better respond promptly, while the person still remembers what he or she has said or done, and before it starts eating us up! How often I would not do that, out of fear that my response would be seen as "unchristian"... and not having the courage to speak up, I hurt both others and myself. Others, because I withheld the truth from them, not correcting them, perhaps even smiling - a fake relationship. I also hurt myself, as it backfired in feelings of depression. For hidden anger will eat us up below the surface. If we seem unable to resolve the situation, we may feel like a failure. We can feel trapped if the situation threatens us. We want to flee and cannot. We may start looking inwardly, in a final attempt to find a solution, and feel guilty. Perhaps we blame ourselves for not being able to handle things, for not being courageous enough, for not having an open relationship no matter how much we pray. If the situation endures, hopelessness can set in and we feel depressed. But a better solution lies in finding the true cause and dealing with it - and that can be a prayerful step of faith. *With the wisdom and help of God, show your righteous anger!* God's anger is righteous and yet He is merciful. He desires restored relationships and reconciliation. He is on our side as we attempt to reach others in truth and love.

F. *Stress and its many faces*. Perhaps you have demanded too much of yourself over a long period of time, or others have placed demands on you that were too heavy. They may have taken advantage of your goodness or expected more than you actually had to give; or you have unsuccessfully kept trying to comply with what others seemed to expect of you. However, you had better not go beyond your own limitations - not doing more than you can handle. There is only so much that you can do. There is only so much that God wants us to do and that He has designed us to do. If we truly go beyond our physical and emotional limitations, or feel pressured to work beyond our Christian convictions, trouble is near. Feelings of despondency can be part of that.

If for many months we have taken no time for ourselves, if going to the birthday party of a friend becomes a tiresome duty, if we did work that proved much too difficult for us or where no encouragement and satisfaction are found, if other people's expectations of us are consistently too high, and also if someone keeps hurting our sensitive spots, then we should sit down and dare to ask ourselves, "What exactly do I find hard in this?". It can be a release to admit that we *do* have limited abilities. We were created with them. It is not a shameful thing - it is truthful to admit that in some respects we lack strength, that we have human sensitivities. It will help us to ask God about this and discuss our findings with a trusted friend. Friends can be a true blessing in this and may help us look in the mirror. God's will for us is good - and He will help us to find it. He will also help us to speak to others who "come on our territory" at work or in our private life with unrealistic demands or overbearing behavior, perhaps in ignorance. Let's be truthful to them, with the loving help of our Lord. They have a right to know why we respond to them in sadness. They will probably help us once they know. As we face these things in times of stress, it also helps to bring about some fundamental changes in our lifestyle, including some relaxing and enjoyable moments every week.

Finally, should you not be able to find the source of your feelings, or if you feel that you are making no progress, then do ask the help of an experienced Christian counselor, perhaps one of the people that you trust and know well. They may have a more objective view of the situation or notice things that you had not thought of yourself. If necessary, they can also help you find professional help.

2.9 Avoid any self-pity and brooding

Self-pity often is a fast road to feelings of depression. The Lord Jesus never felt sorry for Himself, and He had more reasons to... It is good to realize that our feelings are deceptive, and that it is best to think objectively. You may feel very "down", but with the Lord things are still in your favor, because you know Him! We can ask the Lord for His forgiveness when we have allowed self-pity to enter again. Let's not focus on our feelings or our own interpretation of the circumstances, but focus on what the Lord says, also through our common sense. Hold on to Him: the righteous shall live by faith, not by feelings! (Hab.2:4; Rom.1:17; 3:22-24) Therefore, just stop fostering your wounded feelings. You may no longer value life, but God values your life and we can hold onto His Word! That is our strength, as we focus on the objective truth that God is always near, even when we do not sense His presence. He has prepared for us an eternal joy, and we are safe close to Him. Ask Him to show you more of this. No enemy can rob us out of His hands! (Joh.10:29) He understands the very depths of our being and hears our prayers (Rom.8:26-28; 35-39; Ps.138:3; Joh.14:13-14).

Therefore, we do not need to keep focusing on our problems and brooding over them, but we can bring them to Jesus who Himself is the solution. If we start focusing on Him, we grow closer to Him and begin to look more like Him (Col.3:1-4; Eph.4:15; 2.Cor.3:18). Therefore, do not give brooding any room in your thoughts, but occupy them with things that build you up and gladden your heart - like becoming active for a good cause. If our heart is focused on Jesus and His glory, we cannot focus on our problems at the same time. That way, we also learn to stop looking at ourselves and to start making room in our hearts for others and their problems.

2.10 Do not worry about anything (Php.4:6)

Don't let worrying about tomorrow rob us of today's blessing and of being with Jesus. There is no counsel lovelier than this one: to be anxious for nothing, but to pray instead to God who already knows and understands what we are going through. (Mt.6:27-34; 13:22; Lk.21:34-36). This may not always be easy, and if things do go wrong while once again we load the worries upon our own shoulders, we can simply ask Him to forgive us. You can never be relaxed and happy today if worries for the future take away the peace and happiness we find in Him. If fear for the future does have us in its grips, it can help to say to God: "Lord, if that one thing which I fear would indeed happen, then I choose to love You in it and to enjoy Your love for me. I know that even if that situation would arise, You will be my Helper, my Light and my Strength right in the midst of it". It is so safe to know that the future lies in the hands of Him who carries us, and who gives more strength if the circumstances become more difficult.

It is not wrong to make plans for the future - that can even be necessary. But we may daily place the heavy load of it on the shoulders of Jesus. Therefore, if you have worries pray daily to Jesus to help you hand over these worries to Him, and ask Him to give you His joy that day, about all the good things that He gives you. For that is His will - and sometimes we need to choose for that obediently: to enjoy life without worrying!

2.11 Maintaining a healthy lifestyle

A. *Take sufficient exercise, and eat healthy foods*. That may take an effort at times, but it will help us to get on top of things more quickly. Many problems can surface when we become too tense or tired, or when we neglect ourselves. A healthy lifestyle makes it easier for us to face difficult situations. Do not start overeating or drinking when you feel depressed, but eat healthy foods. Many books have been written on this. Some people can get depressed if their sugar intake is too high!

B. *Find things to enjoy.* A regular lifestyle and discipline in your life can indeed help you, and may let you find a regular time during the week for things that you really enjoy. It is so nice and worthwhile to know what these things are! Often we do not even realize them. Find out: what makes you relaxed - cooking? Then you can try to make time for more variation in the menus. Shopping? You may buy some new plants for the garden, or a new outfit. Perhaps you will choose a course you enjoy, or take piano lessons. It is so good to get out of the old rut in our life and start doing something quite different. Often that changes our outlook on life.

C. *Take sufficient rest and leisure time.* When we do not feel like our true selves, we may need to take time to relax and to digest events around us. Stressful times are not the best periods in life to take important decisions that demand a lot from us emotionally. Especially in times of difficult events or bereavement, we need sufficient rest to face things, and we do not do our emotions a favor by pushing away such facts or circumstances by a full agenda or by acting as if nothing happened. It is better to help our emotions cope with life by making sure we have a good rest at night, and by refreshing times like walking or swimming. Running a daily distance or other types of exercise, such as cycling tours or walking the dog, will help improve our physical condition and can bring rest to our spirit as well. That way, we have a "pressure valve" and can better handle life. It seems that jogging helps many people to deal with their feelings of dejection, and especially for people with an office job who sit all day it can bring a refreshing balance.

Finally, if we take times of silence and consciously seek the Lord's help in coping with things, we may find it easier to get through the valleys of life. We may be encouraged to know, that such situations do not last forever and that they often make us more mature people as we learn to lean on God.

D. *Keep visiting relatives and friends.* It is good to take more rest than before, but do not withdraw from contact with others. You render them (or yourself) no service by withdrawing from them. Tell some of your good friends about the burden on your heart, so that they can pray for you and stand with you in these times. Make sure you are dressed well, and keep your house in good order so that your visitors feel welcome. They too need a friend! Try to really keep your appointments. If you visit them, you can bring some flowers. Make them happy, do them a favor - that will also make you happy. It is more blessed to give than to receive (Ac.20:35; 2.Cor.6:10). There is even a special promise of fruit and joy if we bring such a sacrifice and do good while we ourselves do not feel happy: if we sow in tears, we will reap with joy! (Ps.126:5-6).

2.12 Spend a difficult day in a useful way

Try spending the days and times when you feel downhearted on tasks that you do not like. The day is unpleasant anyway, and it's great to vent your frustrations on these dreadful tasks. At the end of the day you can then be glad to notice that, after all, it was a very useful day indeed - many nasty chores done... Also, that way you direct your thoughts to something that in the end has positive results, instead of to things that depress you. A lost day won!

Every person has their own ways of leaving difficulties behind. One may have a time of prayer to tell God all that the heart feels - that can be such a relief! (This, too, can be combined with a healthy, refreshing walk in nature.) Others break away from worrisome thoughts by making a flower arrangement and bringing it to a sick person - and become happy in the process. Moreover, as mentioned before, a good possibility can also be to plan a special hour during the day (or a fixed time in the week) where in the midst of all trouble you can do something nice for yourself that you can look forward to. Then, really hold on to such a time, to help yourself see that life does have its good sides, in spite of all the problems! God so loves us to enjoy life.

2.13 Seek help if you cannot find the way out

Realize that we may allow our heart some time to work through certain events or changes. Allow yourself some time for that. With very deep heartaches, it is not unusual if several months pass before we have worked things through. Perhaps the above has not sufficiently helped you, and you have felt downhearted for a long time. Then: *seek help*! Ask some faithful and reliable Christians who know you well for their advice and prayers, and also go and see your doctor. Perhaps you are experiencing a real depression, or your feelings may be caused by a chemical imbalance in the body - something that medical science has a remedy for.

3
DEALING WITH THE FEAR OF MAN

Fear of man may well be one of the problems most common to man. Even people that you would not expect it from, who may even come across as strong personalities, can suffer from this - perhaps even overcompensating for their insecurity by a self-assured attitude, hoping that no one will notice - perhaps not wanting to admit their fears even to themselves. Others show their weakness more openly. Whatever category we belong to, we can be comforted, for Jesus understands and loves us, He teaches us courage, the true meaning of having "character", and what a strong personality *really* is!

Personally, I always tended to find excuses for this problem; "it was not my fault", I was too young, too weak, had experienced too many difficulties, etc. It is true that Jesus loves us in the midst of our battles and that He helps us in spite of our weaknesses. However, it is still better if we receive healing from this condition.

One day I got to know the fear of man in its true colors, and got a real shock! In my case, the fear of man found its origin in placing the appreciation of other people above the appreciation of God and of what He had created in me! Then, I became serious about this battle; and I did find solutions for this very human problem that others may also benefit from in their own personal situation.

3.1 Changing the direction of our heart

As we direct our heart towards loving the Lord and pleasing Him only, it starts looking away from problems and trying to please people. In fact, *this means a total change of our goals*! It no longer seems important to have or do things to be "in" with the crowd. Many beautiful Scriptures on the "fear of the Lord" (the text points at "reverence for the Lord") will certainly encourage you to direct your heart more fully towards Him, such as Ps.19:10; 25:12-15; 33:18-19; 34:8-20; 61:4-6; 103:13,17; 112:1 etc.; Prov.1:7; 3:6-8; 10:27; 14:26-27; 19:23; Is.11:2-3; Mal.3:16-17; and Acts 10:34-35. If we make Him our first goal, with all the strength we can muster - especially also in situations where we do not feel safe - we will have the only right starting point in the battle. God wants to teach us courage through the "fear of the Lord"; the more we learn to love and obey Him (to "fear" Him), the less space our heart will have left for the fear of man. We simply cannot focus on two opposite things at the same time.

We need not hide our weakness from the Lord Jesus; often the first words He spoke were, "Dot not fear!". He understands the reasons so well. Perhaps people have threatened us in our youth; we may have had some traumatic experiences or were hurt in other ways. We may also need to recognize the guilt of others in this, so that we can forgive them and learn to love them again. This is also important in our relationship with the Lord. Perfect love casts out fear! (1.Jhn.4:18) Some fears originate from a built-in defense mechanism that nature gave us to protect us. If, for instance, an angry armed man comes towards us, fear makes us run away fast to save our life! The Lord has intended that natural kind of fear to be there, so that is not wrong.

However, the fear that this chapter deals with is that for many of us the "fear of man" has started to dominate part of their life. It is always in their thoughts, for instance: fear for the opinion of leaders, for their influence on our life. The Lord wants us to respect and obey those placed above us, thus being a good example (the Bible has a lot to say about the relationship of slaves towards their masters), unless they ask things of us that would displease God. Then we may tell them lovingly that we cannot obey them, explaining why that is so. However, the fear of man can lead us to sin, like when we dare not say "no" when that is necessary, but rather follow others slavishly instead of openly sharing our own opinion or our Christian testimony. Because we are then guided by sinful other people, this can block our growth in trusting the Lord. However, we most certainly can get free from that! The following points may of interest here.

A. *Confess your fears as soon as you notice these*; do not push these fears away. God is always there for us to forgive and help us. If we are scared, we may put our trust in the wrong things, and our trust is not sufficiently in God! For instance, we may think: "If this group or that person accepts me, I am safe"; or: "It would be terrible if they were to notice my weakness". Nothing may be farther from the truth! We are safe through our Lord, in the arms of Jesus - and nowhere else (not even the most courageous person). Yet seeking our security with Him, especially when the circumstances are not easy, may take some time for us to learn. Ask the Lord to heal you of your fears, and to let you grow in trusting the Almighty Father, who in His love wants to protect and help us in every situation. Hold on to His hand, as it were, in all things, and realize that He is close to you.

B. *Take much time to rest in the love of the Lord and to be with Him*. We can keep telling the Lord that we want to know Him more deeply, to love Him and fear only Him; that His gracious and faithful opinion of us is all-important, and that we never again want to give any space to that fear of people and of what they think of us. In the beginning we may often fail - it takes time to change a pattern of thinking that we harbored for years - so it helps to come to the Lord every time we notice those old fears. Let's refuse those any space in our life by bringing them to the Lord.

C. *Pray a lot* - seeking our refuge and security with God - even using that situation to develop a deeper relationship with Him. We can let ourselves be governed by Him, under the control of His will, by the Holy Spirit. He can control us better than we ourselves ever could. That is *the best kind of self-control*! When we experience resistance from other people, we can learn to put our trust in Him and to confide in His love. That is *the best kind of self-confidence*! It is based on His love and faithfulness, not on the love of other people, or on our own frail and sometimes fearful character. As we keep on going His way, we will notice that we start to grow in maturity. Scriptures like 2.Chron.32:8; Ps.23; 27:1-6; 118:8-9; Prov.14:26-27; Is.41:10; 54:11-17; Mt.6:24-34; Jhn.14:27; Rom.8:15; 2.Tim.4:16-17 and Hebr.13:6 may encourage you in this.

3.2 We can decide to break with the fear of man

Making a decision can have a powerful effect! When suffering from "the fear of man" we tend to let ourselves be guided by others and their opinion of us, more than we let ourselves be guided by God and His opinion of us. In other words, we direct our attention to people rather than towards God! (Prov.29:25; Jer.17:5; 1.Jhn.1:5-9) We then tend to put more value on the imperfect and often negative opinion of other people about us and about situations, than on the loving opinion of God. In that sense, we "idolize" people and do what they demand of us just to avoid quarrels, even when this goes against the will of our Lord. We then have more fear of a confrontation than a fear of sin! At times, we are afraid of resisting others and instead try to secure our own position by just talking along with them. Our actions can then become overly submissive, perhaps even cringing. Not only is this a pity (who would choose the fallible opinion of men above the infallible ways of God, the ugly above the beautiful?), but also it can be a step towards sin. Therefore, we need to ask God to forgive us. (Is.8:11-13; Jhn.5:44; Mt.10:28)

Some years ago, when frequently called upon to translate for speakers before in front of people, I initially found that very difficult. Beforehand, I would make sure that all my sins were brought to the cross, that I had prepared the translation work prayerfully, and yet... Continually thoughts would come like: "am I doing this right, do I look right, am I standing here calmly enough, what would people think of me?" - it was all so frustrating! I would stand stiff, translate tensely, and could not hold on to the Lord on top of all that. That battle lasted until one day I heard the advice of a young man who had been so tense doing drama on the street while evangelizing. He testified, "I no longer act for all the people standing there, it makes me too frustrated. No, I now do my acting for the Lord; for He is present too!" Well, I could surely use that idea for translation work - it was just what I had been waiting for. I immediately started using this idea, and would keep the Lord before my eyes who - invisibly - was present among the people. I wanted to do my very best for Him, as His encouraging presence was there. The people could then think whatever they wanted... I would direct my inner eyes so much on Him that everything else went to the background (Ps.16:8). In the beginning, I needed much concentration to do this - but what an essential difference it has made! I learned to put my security in Him. He loves me and accepts me, even when I make a mistake. In the end, He is my goal - not the changing opinions of people around me, even though we may serve them out of the love God gives.

Therefore, we need not become dependent on people, or on our own defenses, but can instead grow in dependency on the Lord. That is *the best kind of self-dependence*! People may not hold us in high esteem, and we may not even esteem ourselves very highly so that we tend to believe their opinion of us. But instead, we may fully accept and hold on to His esteem of us; that is *the best kind of self-esteem*... We may now decide to only fear the Lord and His opinion of us, in awe of Him who loves us so very much!

The fear of man often springs from a negative pattern of thinking and expectation that has developed over the years. Whenever we notice this pattern of fear, we may firmly decide to wage war on it by replacing it with the holy fear of the Lord as we look to Him, and get up with His help. For our fears can influence our actions, and such actions may then not be in line with those God intends for our life... Scriptures like 1.Sam.15:24; Is.30:1-3; 31:1; and Mt.10:24-31 can give us a better view of this.

3.3 Forgiving people who criticize or intimidate us

We will meet people in life who - consciously or unconsciously - focus on our weak spots by intimidation or criticism. Instead of being intimidated, we can then ask the Lord for extra love towards them, and pray for wisdom as to how we can approach them and if He will stand with us in it. These people may have the same problem as we do and perhaps they even try to over-compensate for their insecurity by dominant behavior. It may then help them if we approach them in weakness and without accusation, and take their practical needs into account as well as love them. We are then no longer a threat to them. Especially very difficult people may open up that way!

We can ask the Lord (and people, if we have hurt them) for forgiveness if we, in turn, have also criticized them or intimidated them in order to "be somebody", if we wanted to impress them or to assertively dominate the situation. For then we make the same mistake: we increase and use their fear of man. Thus, we do not respond in the "opposite spirit" of humility that seeks the well-being and healing of the other person. In the end, only the Lord is the One who has the right to rule over any of us. Do we let Him? He is fair and just. We cannot make Him believe that we are better than we really are; but He has a wonderful blueprint of how He intended us and the other person to be - a beautiful plan for which He prepares us!

3.4 Asking for prayer

We can ask God to help us find the right people we can go to for prayer, who know Jesus intimately and who can advise and help us. It is important that they can be fully trusted, so that we can safely confess our weaknesses, sins, and problems. Even just confessing our weaknesses in an atmosphere of trust can be such a relief! If we suffer from the fear of man, such a step may cost us some effort; and it will be a help to know that we have a reliable counselor - one whom we feel God would have us go to. Through several conversations, this person can get to know you better and pray for you. We can then learn to be truly open and transparently honest so that difficulties, wounds, and perhaps wrong attitudes can be healed. The Bible says, that in such a way we can obtain healing from the Lord (Jam.5:13-16).

Generally, fear is a bad advisor. It can bring our thoughts, feelings and motivations into such confusion that it seems harder to clearly see Gods will in our situation. The Lord may then use better advisors: counselors who know Him, who give us His direction through the Holy Spirit (the divine Counselor) and who help us find His guiding hand when we ourselves no longer see things clearly. Such counselors will not make us dependent on themselves, but will help us to depend on the Lord, to stand strong in Him, becoming free of wrong thought patterns and old bondages. In themselves, such counselors are also imperfect, but they can pray for us and speak from their own Christian experience with Gods help.

It can be important to pray that God gives us some friends who know the Lord. As we communicate with people who respect our opinion and who start appreciating us, we will become less vulnerable to people with differing opinions, and thus we learn to develop a healthy measure of trust in others. That can also give us a more balanced view of who we really are (see also Ch.4 & 5) and help us to more quickly get rid of some of that excessive fear of man. We need not feel disturbed if we need some time for this, allowing our emotions to work out these new truths and to act upon them. For so long, our feelings have born the heavy burden of people's hurtful opinions and expectations, that they need some time to grow straight again and to get reoriented by Gods healing, truthful, loving,

and constructive opinion. Therefore, let our thoughts and feelings be permeated by the fact of Gods love and goodness - we can keep speaking this out to our soul until it really sinks in. It needs to hear this important truth!

3.5 Facing our fears eyeball to eyeball!

Do not push your fears to the background any longer. Do not avoid certain people or "fearsome situations" that God would have you face, but look at them intently and ask yourself, what exactly it is that makes you so fearful in them. If we know the real cause, we have found the beginning of the solution.

Perhaps some of us are just overly anxious? In a Concordance we can find Bible verses on anxiety, cares, fears and troubles (such as Php.4:6) that give help and worthwhile advice. Maybe we have an undefined fear of the future? Then it is good to remember: "God loves me, He prepares a place for me in heaven, so that I can be close to Him in all eternity" (1.Pet.1:3-7; Eph.1:18-19). We may dare to look forward to heaven, and take courage from it to fulfill our mission here on earth.

It is especially good to remember, what kinds of people or situations arouse fear in you. It can be helpful to write these down carefully, with some of your thoughts. You can then lay the paper down before the Lord, to ask Him if He will show you the causes of your fear (for instance, painful situations from the past or problems with certain people in your youth). If we remember any of these, we are to forgive all the people involved in it carefully. It is good to take some time for this and do it thoroughly. We then ask the Lord to also forgive us for any negative thought pattern developing from this experience, for instance the misconception that "everybody" would be nasty like that, whilst then we had no good view yet of God's goodness and nearness in our life at the time when these things happened. He so much wants to reveal His compassion and consolation to us! Back then, we may not yet have known that all things work together for good to them that love God (Rom.8:28-29); but now we may ask Him how He saw that situation - through which He intends for us to become even more conformed to the image of His Son. Other Scripture verses that may encourage us in difficult situations are Php.4:13 and Rom.8:31-35. We can pin them up above our bed until we virtually know them by heart. Frequently, that is necessary - for in practice our world of thought must really be "transformed"! (Rom.12:2).

Moreover, let us not be afraid to call the sins of others really "sin" (in our own mind; not to gossip about it to others). We can only truly forgive others when we have admitted that they were guilty. In our fear of man, we often tend to blame only ourselves for what happened; or we inwardly sulk and grieve over it. In both cases, we keep having the problem! If we are truly guilty, we can ask God (and where necessary man) to forgive us; and then forgive ourselves. We can then stand before Him with cleansed robes. However, if we are not guilty, we must put the blame where it belongs and forgive others for their part in wrongdoing. *Forgiveness is a most powerful weapon* in our relationship with others, and especially in our relationship with God who wants to teach us how to forgive.

3.6 How to stop trying to please people

We can avoid becoming too dependent on people and their opinions - we can keep saying in our heart, "Lord, only what You think of me is important" whenever the fear of "what this person might think" gets us in its grip. It is no disaster when others disagree with us, hinder us, and do not invite us to their exclusive circle of friends. It is no drama, even though we may feel it is. We can firmly decide to give room to God's loving thoughts about us - overcoming our feelings of rejection by realizing that God has totally accepted us in Christ, and that we may now accept ourselves as beloved of God, whatever other people think (see Ch.5)! It helps to take time to be with Him who cherishes us. The love of the heavenly Father will make us strong in situations where others reject us. Let's stop seeking our security and comfort in other people, even if we have done so all of our life. There is a much deeper comfort in Jesus! (1.Cor.7:23; Gal.1:10; Col.3:22-24; 1.Thess.2:4-6)

How clearly I remember that day when I had not been personally invited to a birthday party (a custom in my country). It seemed like everybody went there except me.

Perhaps I had simply been forgotten, but my feelings were hurting and I asked the Lord for His advice. Then, in the quietness of the evening, the Lord spoke to my heart. His answer surprised me - He spoke to me from the caption under a photograph in a Christian magazine, where it said that if we go to a quiet place we can experience the most beautiful encounters with Him. I had been so keen to attend that party and the nice group of people, that I had lost view of my most precious Friend who had difficulty even to get my attention. It turned out to be a unexpected and very special evening where I truly met with Him, one that I remember to this day. He really looks forward to that! Afterwards, I was less troubled when uninvited, knowing that my happiness is in the close relationship with the Lord who is always there for me.

If with certain people we do not feel comfortable, or if they do not respect our opinion, they cannot yet become our true friends. Their dislike or disapproval of us is unpleasant, but trying to meet their expectations may well be impossible (except when we have sinned and need their rebuke). Trying to please those who are against us can make our life fruitless, and may make us miss something of the tremendous perspective that God has for us! It is always good to make such situations a matter of prayer. What does God want us to do? We cannot serve both God and man at the same time, and may know that God always loves us - even more so when we feel we are all alone in life. For He is close to the brokenhearted and the sorrowful (Is.57:15, 61:1). He wants to be our best and never failing Friend.

3.7 Making deep obedience to the Lord our priority

Many of us have never quite known how to have or maintain our own opinion; our ideas were swept away only too quickly by intelligent speakers! That often happened to me, and I tended to trim my sails according to the wind. The other speaker would win - because I was not so sure of my own cause. I did indeed have an opinion; but was that really the only truth? However, those who get to know God now have found the unfailing truth of His Word that they can hold on to. Doing so, they learn to become strong soldiers defending the cause of God. Thus, they will also grow in maturity more quickly! That is an extra reason why reading Gods Word should have a very important place in our life. We will then grow not only in strength, but also learn to recognize the truth and to argue our cause against other opinions. This will certainly not please everybody, but God will use it to strengthen our spiritual backbone.

As we learn to take a stand for God, it will especially help us to take our "every thought captive to obey Christ" (2.Cor.10:5-6). As we hold on to His truth, we are working on the "renewing of our mind" (Rom.12:2) and on bringing our thoughts in line with Gods thoughts about us (Ch.9). Thus, we can learn to recognize Gods "good and acceptable and perfect will" in situations around us. Such new thinking can also bring about a deep change in our being!

Therefore, we are to act out of the truth, out of our deepest convictions, out of our faith in the Lord and what He says to us, even if we have to go against the opinions of others or even lose some friends. However, we remain friendly and sensitive to the feelings of others, for we do not want to hurt them - only to express our own opinion clearly. Many of us have not expressed our own opinions when they should have, and for them it is good to give much attention to developing their own preferences and opinion, with the help of the Bible. It is also helpful to frequently ask ourselves, "Now what do I really think about that? Is it right? What are my own ideas? We then guard the personal opinion we have formed. It is something precious that belongs to us, something we have prayed about and that we may be able to bless and enrich others with.

3.8 Daring to be different!

Every beginning is hard, also in these matters. Do we *dare* to be ourselves, to show our own opinions in a group? One situation where we can practice this is when people ask us to join in with something God does not approve of. We then have to show our true colors as children of God, and through the battle we will become strong (Mt.10:32; Ps.144:1-2). By becoming a Christian, we took a stand for God and against sin, and there is nothing that can build up our character as much as the ways in which God, our Teacher, closely leads us through this earthly battlefield with its many tears.

Another growth situation is *evangelism*. Many see this as a risky and difficult activity! There, we stand out as different from those around us; people will notice us and perhaps criticize or scorn us. However, also there people stand alongside us (in prayer, and often in person). We can ask the Lord to give us a deep love for those who are lost, and can pray for them whenever He brings them to mind. Pray also, when and where you may join an evangelism activity, and for Him to prepare you. We may always pray for His grace and for the power of His Holy Spirit, Who longs to reach out to people, as our boundless resource of confidence and boldness! (Eph.6:18-20; 1.Thess.2:1-8)

3.9 Letting others feel safe with us

From our own experience, we know how awful it is to wrestle with the fear of man. That means: we give to others what you would desire for ourselves - in security, in space to be themselves. Try to make them feel confident and at home (Mt.7:12, Is.58:10), and learn to listen. Put relationships and hospitality high on your agenda (Ch.7 & 8). Take good notice if people around you are fearful in certain situations or if they feel threatened. Stand next to them, even if unnoticed and just in your thoughts; defend them, protect them, love them, and pray for them. We may not be very good at this in the beginning, but we can train ourselves in this and try to find (even in the long run) if there is an opening to tell them of our own battles, and the lessons that God is teaching you and me in the midst of it. Always take them seriously, respect them even if they may not have learned to respect themselves; and never be ashamed of them. God is not!

We can also learn to act out of the "opposite spirit" towards the people that we feel threatened by: reaching out to them in openness, meekness, prayerful wisdom, and forgiveness.

Let's not avoid such a "difficult" person, as they may feel rejected and defend themselves even more. We may not learn these lessons very quickly, but they are very worthwhile. Remember: people with the largest and most threatening defense mechanisms are often the most insecure inside (the weaker the city, the stronger the walls); the defense is only to make sure nobody will notice how vulnerable they really are or how much they long for appreciation!

It may also help us to remember the words of Jesus, "Love your enemies, and pray for those who persecute you" (Mt.5:44). Love is a mighty weapon; moreover, "perfect love casts out fear" - both in them and in us. (1.Jhn.4:18-21) If we remain close to the Lord, abiding in His love, He teaches us to love others (Rom.5:5). Love is not merely a feeling, but a choice to seek the best for the other person and to keep blessing him or her (of course, warm feelings can result from this). It may take a lot of courage to love others and to speak to them, but *especially in fear, courage manifests itself*. If a situation does not threaten us, we need no courage and cannot exercise ourselves in that. However, some situations can be very difficult and threatening. We need not forcefully take these things upon ourselves, but can keep trying to love the other person in practical ways and to quietly make the choices God wants us to - even if these are not popular with those around us.

Obedience to God is a mighty weapon against the fear of man! In this, too, it is more blessed to give than to receive. One day we may harvest what we have sown, not only in our own lives but also in the healing of others. Jesus in His love won the battle by never giving up!

4
ADVICE ON INSECURITY

Most of us know what it is to feel insecure. In some situations, we may not feel safe in what we do or in who we are. We may often believe that other people can do a better job, we fear to give a poor show ourselves, or that we might not be accepted for who we are. We may not even be sure that we accept ourselves! We can shrink away from people that come across as very "self-assured" - but remember: *a better kind of self-assurance* comes from our assurance that God is on our side to help us, that He accepts us;- let our assurance stem from our relationship with Him - and that is something for which we can pray.

Many of us first want to get used to new situations and get familiar with new people there before we feel safe enough to express our opinions. There certainly is wisdom in that! However, if we strive for perfection we can fall short of our own expectations for the high level of achievement that we had wanted to reach. We become disappointed with ourselves (and frequently with others who do not live up our standards either). Are we trying to live a perfect life *in our own strength*? At the same time, it is precisely because of our high standards that we often serve God with commitment and conscientiously, which brings joy to His heart.

The reason for feelings of insecurity can differ from person to person, but perhaps some people can benefit from the thoughts below.

4.1 Developing an intimate relationship with the Lord

God is our strength and our security; with Him we are safe in every situation (Ex.15:2-3; Ps.63:1-8; 139:1-6; Prov.14:26;

Jhn.10:28-30). He has created us and knows what we are made of; He knows what plans He has for me and you (Jer.29:11-13). He Himself is the final goal of our future; and He is the only One who can honestly prove our heart and tell us what to do.

Just thank Him every day that He lives within you in all His glory, since you invited Him into your heart on the day you were converted (Jhn.17:22-23; 1.Jhn.4:4,13-16; Rev.3:20). Nothing is impossible with God; He has every situation in His mighty hand (Mt.17:20; Lk.1:37; Ps.65:7). Wherever we go, He goes with us to encourage, help and comfort us. We can offer Him the throne of our heart and ask for His advice any time. We need not try to struggle on our own, or to control the situation, but can live in openness and worship before Him. He will fight for us, and we have only to be still (Ex.14:14; Ps.46:7-10; Ro.8:31). If we allow Him to cleanse our heart regularly and to develop an intimate relationship with us, our life will bear fruit whatever the circumstances, and whatever people may think of us (Jhn.15:4-5). With Jesus, we are always safe, and He longs to be our Friend.

4.2 "I feel so guilty and imperfect"

The best help is to make sure that our sins have been forgiven and left behind. We can just come to Jesus every time and confess our sins, accepting His forgiveness and His friendship. Our real security lies in our personal relationship with God, our Helper. Nothing should tarnish that relationship, so we will try to daily bring our sins to Him - and ask for His forgiveness and cleansing (Hebr.10:17-23,35; 13:18; Php.3:9-10). We can then worship Him and pray with a cleansed heart, without the accuser trying to whisper in our ears that we are not good enough to come to God and have our prayers answered! It sounds so simple, but sometimes we really need to work at it - to be open to confess our own faults, to consciously accept God's forgiveness through Jesus, and to clearly tell the enemy to leave when he starts accusing us again of our old and already forgiven sins. Be very strict with him!

How do we deal with feelings of guilt? From my own experience, I know these can be very bothersome. I so much desired to walk with the Lord, and yet mostly felt so guilty and imperfect. Whenever I prayed about it, even more imperfections would come to mind that I brought to the Lord. The "big sins" had been confessed some time ago, and yet the sinful heart they had come from was still there - or so I thought. Let me share the way I found to get rid of these problems...

(A) I realized that the Bible clearly teaches about forgiveness of sins. Being accused of my old sins should not be necessary, and yet it kept happening, on and on! Therefore, I took a notebook, and every day wrote down what I had asked forgiveness for, writing them down with the date and specific aspects. I asked forgiveness for all sins that entered my mind (long lists – even including accusations from the enemy that I did not always discern as such), just in case anything about it was true. Then, I consciously accepted God's forgiveness, thanking Him for it. That, too, I wrote down (this is something we can do every day) - and soon I noticed something ... at times I felt guilty about sins which God had already forgiven! It was there, a few days before, in my notebook! Well, that was an accusation from the enemy. Then I could say: Go away, accuser, in the name of Jesus Christ who died in my place and Who has paid for these sins! I kept saying this, insisting on it, now fully convinced of the lies about me that the enemy had whispered in my ears. It went on like this for quite some time. I kept confessing what came to mind, except when I knew I had fully confessed that same sin before and could rest in His forgiveness. Thus, I did learn to consciously accept forgiveness and to send the accuser away.

(B) After this time in my life, my feelings of guilt would often be vague: "You know you are bad, or you would not have done all those things in the past". There was little or nothing specific that I could confess to Jesus and be forgiven for by Him. The enemy was probably out of fuel but did not want to admit it and kept trying: he whispered that I simply *was* bad, that's why those sins had occurred in the past, even though the ones I had confessed were now forgiven. Because of this, the cloud of guilt, in a thinner form, kept hanging over me. Of course, I was imperfect… If people even looked at me in a negative way, the cloud would become heavier again: Had they noticed wrongs in me that I did not even know about myself? The battle against guilt remained, yet on a different level. It took a while before I found the solution.

Being "in Christ"

During Bible College years, I had heard about the "in Christ concept" and started studying all phrases in the New Testament where the words "in Christ" occurred. This is something I would recommend to everyone with problems in this area! For it is "in Him" that we are fully accepted by God, that we have a divine wisdom, righteousness, sanctification and redemption (1.Cor.1:30-31), and not by anything that I could do myself. The big question was: what did it mean, being "in Christ"? Then, in my search, I came across some marvelous words in 2.Cor.5:17 - *I was a new creation through my personal relationship with Jesus*! Could that be true - was I not the old guilty self who just happened to find a forgiving Friend? Could I truly hide in Christ? It was one of the most daring decisions I had to make: to accept that what God says is true, that indeed I was now a new creation through my relationship with Jesus, who had cleansed me from both old and very recent sins. There is no more condemnation for those who are "in Christ Jesus" (Rom.8:1). I had to consciously accept it and defend it against my own bad feelings about myself! In the end, it worked…

After this, our thoughts need no longer be worried and concerned about old sins. For we realize that God accepts us in every respect - that He hears our prayers on the basis that Jesus has borne our guilt and punishment. This is the only way that we can learn to stand in faith, with a clean conscience, especially when the enemy or other people accuse us. We are a new creation "in Christ" – do we still nurture a loving relationship with Him, as our priority?

(C) It is also important that we learn to test the opinion of people around us against the opinion of God! For sometimes they are right, and we may indeed have sinned - for instance at a moment when we got angry with someone and did let go of Jesus' hand... That is something that we may pray for discernment about. Just ask forgiveness of God and man, as soon as we can, so that the accuser (the devil) no longer has any hold on us. Feelings of guilt should not be pushed away but dealt with, so that we can truly be free of them.

After consciously receiving forgiveness, the certainty that we are no more under condemnation (Rom.8:1) may only dawn on us slowly, because most of us are led by our feelings: "I still feel just like before", rather than by the facts and the security of God's Word that He has forgiven and cleansed us of our sins. Our feelings have been deformed by the world and by sin and are often unreliable, but they can be healed if we keep telling our worrying soul of the truth of God's Word, of His acceptance of us, and of His forgiveness of sins (Eph.1:4-7; Col.1:12-14). For through God's forgiveness we are clothed in a white and spotless garment! Realizing this will aid the inner healing that many of us need so badly.

(D) When all of the above has not sufficiently helped us to get rid of our feelings of guilt, we can ask a mature Christian whom we trust for prayer. The Bible tells us in James 5:16 about confessing our faults to one another, and the effect of the fervent prayers of the righteous (see also Mt.18:16). If we can find no one or have no courage, we may try to go to a Christian conference or to another church or city. Let us make sure we settle this matter and get rid of the sins and guilt that Jesus paid for by His own blood...

4.3 Bring everything to the Lord at the beginning of the day

Insecurity about our own abilities can also work to our advantage. Then, we will more readily ask for God's guidance in all experiences and relationships and concerns that we will encounter during the day ahead. He wants to be our Friend. We don't need to go through the difficulties in our own strength; we can ask for His blessing and presence through all that happens during the day. He wants to fulfill His plans for us in it. Whatever we do in total abandonment and obedience to the Lord Jesus is under the responsibility of our Creator. He knows exactly what our gifts and talents are, and what things we may not be able to do of ourselves. If we fail, or if people criticize us, we can find full forgiveness, strength, and comfort with Him. Then, the remarkable thing is that we start getting to know Him better in everyday life and to grow in maturity. Trusting God is so much better than trusting in yourself. Insecure people do not always trust in themselves - and that is their strength if they start trusting in God! (2.Cor.12:9-10) *The best kind of self-reliance* is to rely on the almighty God who loves and strengthens us. We no longer need to rely on other peoples' ideas or faith, or on our own limited strength, but can experience God's peace in every situation, because we allow Him to take us by the hand and guide us.

Do we feel that our views are not respected or even recognized by others? It may help to make a list of such opinions. We no longer conceal these, but we pray about them and (if we feel they stand the test) admit to ourselves that our opinion is indeed important. Then, we can ask God for freedom and boldness to speak out at the right time (Eph.4:14-16; 6:18-20). We thus learn to fight for issues that we feel are important! That way, our ideals can become a reality, our gifts and talents can be used, and we may also be tested: others may not always agree with us! If we remain open to them, we mature and learn new things.

4.4 Promoting our true maturity

A. We can promote our spiritual health and growth by seeking the Lord frequently and spending time with Him, thus strengthening our relationship with Him. (2.Pet.3:18). Let us praise and thank Him often; it is so good to be with Him! Our faith will also increase by reading Gods Word regularly, by prayer, by regularly listening to good Christian speakers, and by relationships and discussions with other

Christians. Thus, we will stand stronger in our faith and be less susceptible to whatever the world thinks of us. Our strength will then no longer lie in other people's opinion but in God's opinion of us, and in the confirmation of friends who also know the Lord Jesus personally. That way, we no longer direct ourselves to the world, but to the expectations of our Lord.

We will reflect the things we keep looking at! The more we become conscious of the faithfulness, love and beauty of the heavenly Father, the more this will radiate out of us and encourage those around us (2.Cor.3:18; 4:6-7).

B. Another and very practical exercise for growth is: *greeting others with interest*. This can be a worthwhile exercise towards more relaxed contacts with other people. Many of us can at times be shy and only greet the other person superficially. Now a greeting is something that we do anyway, but we can give it something extra! It is a beautiful exercise, for it is a "safe form of contact" that may even be expected of us. No one will be surprised if you greet them a bit more extensively - at the most people think "he or she seems in a good mood today". If you hardly know the person, keep your greeting friendly and look at them intently. That is, "in the eyes"! As you greet them, bless them in your heart (with a silent prayer). In the beginning, such greetings may not be easy; but if you make a point of doing this, you will start noticing the difference. Last, but not least, it will make you grow in freedom and boldness! If you know the person somewhat better, than you can have a brief conversation with them. Do not go any further than your courage takes you, but do pray to the Lord that He will bless and multiply what you do for Him in such contacts; people are very important to Him.

Perhaps some of us do not find these things easy at all, but we can start with the people that we know well (relatives, neighbors and people at work), or even with those who do not know us at all and who may never meet us again. You may also find that many older people have much time and enjoy brief conversations! Tasks like pouring coffee at church events will also make greeting others easier. It will help both you and others if you are available for such duties more frequently.

4.5 No more performance-oriented

Many of us want to really achieve something in the hope of being accepted and loved by others, for then we also find it easier to accept and love ourselves. To that end, we often try to achieve "our own goals" in which God does not take the initiative. However, if our feelings of security lie in popularity, in being clever, in wealth, or even in being accepted by friends, we will inevitably be disappointed. To God, however, it is not important what we are but *who* we are. We are not necessarily what other people think we are, but who God thinks we are as a person. He knows! He knows our personality, our honesty, and in how far the fruit of the Holy Spirit has started to grow in us (Ps.139:1-6; Gal.5:22-23) – and *this fruit develops when we focus on God*! A deep personal relationship with Him results, in which He can share His plans and goals for our life, instead of our plans to fulfill all sorts of expectations. We then need no longer be disappointed by our "old nature" (whatever other people think), but keep coming to Him for forgiveness and renewal of that intimate relationship with Him. It is absolutely wonderful to know that we *are* a new creation in Christ, through that relationship (2.Cor.5:17-18). By having all our sins washed away - however recent, however small - and by the continuous relationship with Him, we may know that we are holy and filled with His fullness! (Eph.3:19; Php.1:11; Col.1:21-22; 2:9-10). He lives in us; His Holy Spirit empowers us...

Frequently, performance-orientation results from an unfulfilled desire for love and appreciation; but the love we really seek cannot be found that way. Human efforts can work in us an imbalance between pride (wanting to achieve) and humility (failing to achieve). Sometimes, we hope that our insecurity will leave by a better performance - yet such perfectionism makes us even more insecure as we keep failing to achieve our own high standards! Our feelings can swing back and forth between "I do not perform as I should" and "the *other* person achieves less than my standards demand" (this perfectionism, born from insecurity, can make us proud and critical towards others who fail to perform). That way, we end up under the law, not under the grace of Jesus Christ who forgives our sins and imperfections, who accepts us in all our weakness, who loves and appreciates us. If in our lives we are not fully aware of these glorious facts, we cannot convey them to others. Instead, we take upon ourselves the guilt of our failure: "It is my own fault, I fail to achieve" (and we keep trying to do better), and perhaps we now use the same measuring rod with which we have measured ourselves, to measure others. Believe me, they will fail, too! Moreover, they will instinctively feel that we do not build them up in love, while they may not realize that we are using that same high standard for ourselves, because in our own insecurity we hope no one will criticize us if we can just perform well enough. Thus, they cannot see how - deep inside - such "performers" really long for their love. Start loving the perfectionists - it can be a healing experience for them! (Perhaps it would help them if you do not clear up the mess in your house too perfectly before inviting them over... and it might help you, too.)

It is easy to see how our own perfectionism can make the other person insecure, too - and that way we harvest in others what we have sown from our own insecurity! Isn't it wonderful, that God accepts us as we are, and not for what we achieve. All those achievements in the eyes of others are not necessary. His security and love are already there!

The big question now is: do we choose our warm and loving God first of all, or do we seek the favors of others?

4.6 Praying about the causes

It can be quite worthwhile discovering the causes of our insecurity and, possibly, of our negative self-image. We can think of the kind of situations in which we feel most insecure and ask the Lord what circumstances and people could have triggered or contributed to these feelings (for instance, painful situations as a young child, in the family, at school, in relationships, etc.). If anything comes to mind, we can jot this down in a list. Then, one by one, we pray through this list, and *forgive* all who were involved in that specific situation. We can stop pushing that old pain away, instead forgiving those people for the different ways they have hurt us and for the consequences that resulted in our later life. It helps to speak out before God that we will renew and if possible deepen our decision to forgive these people if such memories return later on. Let the choice to forgive be a firm one. We can do this with our mind and will; it may take a few weeks before our negative emotions start changing (Ch.5(3)). If in the beginning we "feel" nothing, this certainly does not mean that we have not truly forgiven! It can take some time for forgiveness to be fully worked out in our emotions. If the pain of such an old situation has not totally gone yet, it can be good to pray about it once again and to keep telling the Lord of our decision to forgive; and to pray for those involved - especially if we remember some painful details that we have not forgiven them for yet. Learning to forgive will be healing to our own soul.

In this process, forgiveness can become a deep habit, like breathing! Painful memories can start to depart, thus promoting our healing. Let's pray for each person on our list to be deeply blessed by God.

As we obey the Lord in all these things, we break down the old, rickety foundation of our feelings (a breeding ground for bitterness, wounded reactions, and hardness of heart) and make the ground ready for a new attitude of heart, restoration of relationships, and the building of a "new house" for our personality, of which God is the Architect.

4.7 Appreciating what God created when He made us

We can choose to respect ourselves in daily events. It can be helpful to write down just what negative things our old feelings believed about ourselves (deep inside) and be truly honest! Then, compare these with the positive things God says about you. He loves you, He Himself created you, and He saw that it was very good! (Gen.1:31; Ps.139:13-17;

2.Cor.5:16-17). We are very precious to Him and honored (Is.43:4), so much so that he allowed His Son to die for you and me, that we might inherit eternal life. It is important that we realize with our mind, based on God's Word and Jesus' forgiveness (see Ch.4.(2)) that we are pleasing to God. If we keep degrading and punishing ourselves with negative thoughts, it will be hard to believe that God does indeed accept us - for He holds you and me you in high esteem. Let's not under-estimate God's creation...

Therefore, we can resist lies and negativity about ourselves that may have held our thought life in their grips for too long, and which the enemy might use to depress us. We need not accept these any longer! We can simply ask God to forgive us for our not yet having accepted that He created us for a truly beautiful purpose! That way, our faith can grow. Often, the rickety old thought patterns have developed over the years, but they will certainly be broken down if we firmly decide to exchange such lies with the truth of God's intense goodness: for He takes pleasure in us and loves us. Let us look at the beautiful qualities that He has given us, so that we learn to accept and appreciate ourselves. This takes a radical choice, but it is so worthwhile! It helps to spend a lot of time to discover these. By looking at yourself differently, you will notice that others too will start looking at you differently (more on this in Ch.5, 6, and 9).

With the Lord, we need not be ashamed of our insecurity. He uses what is weak to put to shame what is strong (2.Cor.12:9-10), and it can even be an advantage to know that we are weak, as then we are less inclined to seek our securities within ourselves. Thus, our insecurity can make it easier for us to find our strength in God (1.Cor.1:30-2:5).

4.8 Receiving courage and strength

We can pray to God daily for the empowering of the Holy Spirit, God's power source for every Christian. We do not need to walk the Christian path of life alone, but may lean on Him who redeemed us and who sent the Comforter to go with us, even in our ordinary daily life.

The Holy Spirit also wants to give us boldness (Ac.1:8; Eph.3:12,16; 6:10-20). I have seen shy and insecure people change deeply after the infilling (baptism) with the Holy Spirit! That can become a continual reality in our life. If the Lord has given us a spiritual gift as listed in 1.Cor.12 (for instance, a new language or musical gift), it can be a source of strength to us to use these as often as possible in our daily duties and circumstances (1.Tim.4:14; 2.Tim.1:6-9; 1.Pet.4:10-11).

Scriptures like Ps.27:1-6; Prov.3:25-26; Is.35:3-4a; Neh.8:10; Jhn.14:26-27; Php.4:13; and Hebr.11:34 (there are many more in a concordance!) show that God is our strength and our protection. It is always worthwhile to write down some of the most beautiful Scriptures we can find and pin these up above our desk. We can also permeate our thoughts with Gods truth by learning some verses by heart which especially strengthen us.

4.9 Encouraging others

As we know from experience how insecurity and discouragement can weaken our lives, almost nothing is as wonderful as learning to encourage others, if the Lord gives us an opportunity to do so. This is not too risky and a very rewarding task! The world needs so much encouragement. Perhaps we ourselves have missed much encouragement, and so we can more easily recognize the feelings of insecurity in others and sympathize with them. Insecure people can be sensitive and easily hurt; but the Holy Spirit may want to put your sensitivity to good use to strengthen and encourage them.

Therefore, if we can identify with the feelings of others, we can ask God to help us develop this valuable gift of encouragement to help them and build them up. Just ask Him how you can encourage others; then do what is in your heart - visit them, show them your affection, bring some flowers, a card with a Scripture verse that you have prayed for. Never fail to compliment them whenever you notice good and positive things in them. We can look out for people who need encouragement. What would have encouraged *you* in their circumstances? We can comfort them with the comfort with which we ourselves have been comforted by God (2.Cor.1:3-7). That way, even our insecurity and problems can work together for good in His kingdom... (Rom.8:28) The Lord says that it is more blessed to give than to receive (Ac.20:35). Therefore, we may sow in obedience those encouragements that we may have longed for so much in our own life, and let them take root in the lives of others, now that we have seen how very valuable they are. We will reap with joy! (2.Cor.9:6-10; Ps.126:5).

5
WHAT TO DO ABOUT LOW SELF-ESTEEM

We need not be ashamed to look at ourselves! Low self-esteem can result from wounds and blows that we have received in past circumstances, mostly those in our childhood when we did not have the insights to defend ourselves sufficiently.

As insecurity and a negative self-image are related, it may be good to first read the previous chapter. This chapter is intended as an extra help to those wrestling with a low self-esteem, and it may help us to try out some of the thoughts below.

5.1 The heavenly standards

Rather than being impressed by the opinion of the world about us, it is good to make sure to only use Gods standards for our life as found in the Bible (e.g. Mt.7:1-5; 2.Cor.10:12-18). Throughout our lives, the world tries to fill the "library of our heart" with its own standards and measures: we ought to be intelligent, trained, modern, successful, well-to-do, of good appearance, etc., to "be someone" and to be appreciated. In the past, the cupboards of our heart have been filled with the world's dusty files containing all sorts of expectations and courses we might take to qualify for people's acceptance and to belong to them.

When we compare ourselves with the "in" crowd of this world, we may feel unworthy, as if our opinions do not count because we are not good enough for them and have to strive and perform to be accepted and loved, to work on developing our personality, etc. Such demands become a burden to us, and yet we can find it so hard to cast them off, hoping that one day "the world" may still accept us. What a trap of the enemy! Even if we do all of these things, we will still notice that it will never be enough, that we will always fail somewhere, if only because one cannot please everybody. I write this down as someone who has really tried these things - but in the end, it does not satisfy. Our self-acceptance and sense of self-worth will not develop that way, for we remain conscious of our shortcoming according to the standards of the world. We will keep running faster and faster to be accepted, not knowing that the world's race has no finish... We will never seem good enough, and this way proves to be a dead alley, because in spite of it's promises the world has so little love to offer.

Yet we can take a firm decision: to throw all those dusty files with worldly standards and measures out of the cupboards of our heart, and to start using God's measures instead. As the Creator of the universe whom we serve, He is the only one who truly knows our value. *True self-acceptance* comes from deeply resting in Gods acceptance and love for us; *true self-sufficiency* comes from resting in the Almighty Who is sufficient to care for us. He has beautiful expectations for our life! In His eyes we are so infinitely precious and loved (Jer.29:11; 1.Cor.1:27-28; Jam.2:5). We can choose to no longer receive our sense of value from people, however enticing that may seem. Having rigorously emptied our "cupboard" of those standards, we can then ask God to cleanse it and to fill it with the truth of His love and His perfect advice for our life. He has created you and me as precious and highly esteemed people with a unique range of possibilities, repeated nowhere else in the world in the same way (Is.43:1-4; 54:11-14). If we open ourselves to Him and His power, He can use us in a way the world knows nothing about.

The world may not esteem us very highly, but *true self-esteem* comes as we let ourselves be esteemed by our heavenly Father. The world may not see our worth, but *true self-worth* comes from letting our worth be settled by our loving Creator. The world may not have a good opinion of us and hold us in contempt, but God's opinion (not even our own feelings) is what really counts as the *true basis of our opinion of ourselves.*

5.2 Discovering our sufficiency in Christ

We have been created as unique beings. Therefore, it is important to stop comparing ourselves with others. It may help us to ask, "Do I really feel of less value? Less than what people? In what?" Try to find real answers here. If we look at this objectively, we will see that others can sometimes do things better than we do but that they, too, have their weaknesses. Perhaps they have learned better to live out of the gifts they *do* have, rather than out of the gifts they are missing when they compare themselves to others... and that can make their talents come across more clearly. It is futile to try to become just like the other more popular person; that way, we throw away our own uniqueness. However, it is a different thing altogether to be challenged by their holy lifestyle! Within our circumstances, we can find our own ways to incorporate what we esteem in their lifestyle. It is good to be challenged by them - yet we do not need to copy all they do. God has a special outline and blueprint for our own life, and it differs from that of other people's lives. In short, by trying to become just like other people, we may fail to recognize the unique things God has given us, and may even throw them away!

The plan that God has in mind for our life will fit in with our gifts and personality, but He has little opportunity to develop these if we keep measuring ourselves by the standards of other people (sometimes even our fellow-Christians), trying to develop gifts that we do not really have - and getting discouraged when that does not work! For then our energy will be spent on acceptance and success in the world, rather than seeking out and developing those things God intends for us. In itself, it is not wrong to strive for success if this is directed towards His will for our life, to His glory and to the increase of His kingdom. Even then, true success can only come if we are deeply motivated by the desire to please Him rather than ourselves or people around us. Standing in the "first love to Jesus" is of more value than all gifts combined.

So often I received a blessing from an old Dutch song that says, *"Nothing remains here on earth ... but whatever has been done out of love for Jesus, that is what will keep its value forever"*. True economy!

By loving Jesus, our motivation will naturally change direction - no longer to find our value from people, to safeguard our own position, or to avoid problems that stem from the negative opinion of others. Our motivation is then anchored in our love and obedience towards the Lord. Insecure as we are, this is a true sacrifice of giving up some old "earthly securities" - but, in return, we will receive real and heavenly securities in the relationship with our loving God! This is *true self-security*. We can only experience this if we try living with Him and practicing these things, and we will find that He is sufficient for our needs. He is our only reliable Source of safety and security if we fail or are weak, and we will experience His deep joy when we act on His instruction and with a desire to honor Him! (1.Cor.1:26-30; 2.Cor.12:9-10).

Now what can be our attitude, if we meet people who can do things so much better than we can?

A. *Let's not be jealous* (confess it if you are, asking God to forgive you). Grant them the qualities that God has given to them (you may even need them one day). Give them a wholehearted compliment when they do well, if you find an occasion to do so! If we cannot yet do that, this may mean that we have not fully gotten rid of our jealousy yet. We can go to the Lord and ask for His forgiveness and advice once again. He is our Friend even as we are in the midst of our battle against jealousy. It is a nasty enemy, with which we can unknowingly hurt other people. Our jealousy makes that they blossom in our presence...

It will help us in our battle to seriously start noticing the loving things God says about us personally! He appreciates our personality more than we do it ourselves (remember, He created us!), and He intensely loves us. Have we ever made the choice to love ourselves? Love is a conscious choice, not simply a feeling (feelings are mostly results of our choices and thought life). If we feel we are unlovable, we hold our loving Creator to be a liar. He even gave up His own Son to pay for our sins, because He loved us! It will greatly help us to realize that He fully accepts us and to rest in Him, content with what we have. Scriptures that can help us when we are jealous are e.g. Ps.37:1-8; 73:1-17; Prov.23:17-18; Gal.5:25-26; 1.Tim.6:6-8; Hebr.13:5-6.

B. *Look well at how uniquely God has created* that other person, how beautiful His work is. Thank Him for it, and know that the same Master has created you as a unique and special being, with possibilities that no one on earth has in the same way! When we start being spontaneously happy for others who are doing things well, we may know that we have also started placing our own identity in the Lord (we start to believe that the loving things He says about us are true, and not what others or even we think about ourselves). It can change our life.

C. *Start thanking the Lord for your own gifts and talents,* which He gave to you, and stop directing yourself towards gifts that He gave to others. Perhaps you have not fully discovered what gifts the Creator has given you (it can be exciting to start discovering these!), but His plan and gifts for your life are just as unique and beautiful as the ones He gave to others around you. Or do you just dismiss your own gifts with the thought "that's nothing special"? We are so much used to our own gifts and talents, that we believe these are "normal", that probably everyone has these (they just don't talk about it, right...?). We may not even notice our own gifts any more! Do we make an effort to discover, appreciate, and develop what He has already given to us, or do we keep staring at others who took the trouble to discover and develop their own gifts? They, too, had to make an effort; they, too, have a cross to bear in life in spite of their talents; they, too, need God's strength to walk through life. Don't just look at the outside glitter. Start appreciating and loving them!

While still in school, I often was envious of others who did well in sports (a skill I very much lacked). Those were the popular people, that counted in our group. With volleyball games, I was often among those last selected, and that did not help my low self-esteem... Every sports lesson was a blow to it. The reason was that I had put my worth in the opinion of others, and in how they esteemed my pitiful achievements. I did not realize the tremendous worth that God in His love saw in me. So I felt as if I did not count, was second-rate. The fact, for instance, that I had a good set of brains and a reasonable singing voice did not seem to count. Instead, I had to really learn to place my self-esteem in God's opinion of me! My achievements in sports have certainly not improved, but now I shrug my shoulders and think, "Well, the Lord loves me, and He has given me other talents". *Do not underestimate God's creation in you.* The opinion of other people then becomes much less relevant. It is a choice you will have to make. Who will you believe in - God or sinful man? When we know how much God appreciates us, and when we start appreciating the gifts He gave us, we will be less likely to envy others, and more prone to let them outshine us in the talents God has given them - for His own glory and for the Body of Christ.

D. *Give much room to others and their talents* - the room you would have wanted for yourself. Bless them, and pray that their gifts may be put to good use in God's Kingdom, so that He receives the glory for it. For them, too, He gave the Scripture that they should let their light shine before men, so that they would give glory to Him (Mt.5:16). Perhaps they will outgrow you and become more prominent (even though they may be younger!) in God's Kingdom. God gives them all the room to do so - do we? Do we give them all opportunity to build His Kingdom and to glorify Him? Can we truly thank God for them and their work? Do we pray for wisdom in helping them become what He has in store for them?

5.3 How to find true acceptance in God

Most of us know with our mind that God accepts us in Christ, through the forgiveness of our sins that Jesus paid for. Nevertheless, for many, even though they have confessed their sins, this remains a "mind matter" for too long! Our feelings seem to believe differently. God would so much like us to take time to enjoy His love and acceptance (Eph.1:5-7; Ps.91) and all that we find in His presence. Let's find a quiet corner and take time to sit at His feet. He wants to hear our voice, to hear us ask for His will for our life. He enjoys it if we start finding and developing the gifts and talents He gave us, that fit into the special plan He has for us. God *is* love, and we need to realize that! Often we think that God is far away or are terrified when we think of Him. As long as we do not eradicate this lie from our thoughts, we will find it hard to accept His love! It's easy then to fall into the trap of looking for worldly imitations, becoming dependent on people for the love we need. If we start trying to please people to win their acceptance, we cannot fully be a servant of Christ (Gal.1:10; 1.Cor.7:23). If we receive our much needed love from our relationship with God, as we spend time with Him, then we can truly fill our love reservoir and also hand out from that love, rather than being dependent on other people for it.

One way in which we can receive the love of the Lord is by - as it were - *sitting on His lap*. It is still "safe in the arms of Jesus"! This will also help us eradicate the lie that God, whom we may call "our Father", would not be love... Personally, it took me quite some time to truly believe that God was love, because my feelings said otherwise (Ch.9(4)). During my days with Youth with a Mission, I asked prayer for this problem. Then a young Christian in our prayer group took courage and told me that I believed in a lie! I was shocked - but it was so true. I had acted out of some wounded feelings, and not out of God's truth. Our feelings can be so unreliable, deformed by a world of sin and by wounds from our past - or perhaps by some negative examples given by our own imperfect parents (such as an overly strict dad; with young children, the role of the father can play an important role in how we feel about God). A negative example by others or difficult experiences can make us develop a negative expectation pattern. I did understand some of this, yet did not know what I could do about it. But that I had believed in a *lie*, that was a shock! I asked the Lord to forgive me for believing that He would not truly love me, and later on forgave all those people in my life who by their deeds might have caused some of that negative expectation pattern in my feelings.

A lesson in Lebanon

Now, lets us take a small detour to an event in my life that happened just a few weeks later and that showed me an important key on how to deal with my imperfect feelings. During my time in Youth With A Mission (Heidebeek, The Netherlands) we lived close to a military zone where every Tuesday or so the soldiers practiced shelling. That was quite a normal thing; we knew what was going on and it almost felt familiar. However, during an outreach in Lebanon in 1983, we heard much shelling as different Muslims and Druze groups fought either each other or the Christians. These unexpected events and the shelling did not disturb us too much - the sound was so familiar! However, then I noticed how I kept telling my feelings: Watch out, this is not normal, this is *war*!!! Find a safe place! After several weeks, I was shaken to the core when shelling sounds occurred. My mind had taught my heart to respond in a certain way, by frequently speaking to it about danger, and I reaped the results in my feelings: fear! Even more striking was that when I returned home, the sound of soldiers who practiced now shocked me to the core. Even a slamming door left me trembling. It was interesting to hear my own self-talk when that happened: "This is just nothing, we are back in the Netherlands now; there is no war here and you know it!" Once again, I kept telling my heart what to do - and after just over a month, the fear left me.

Now, as seen above, during this time I was fervently looking for ways to believe and receive God's love (see Ch.9(4)). So, in my desperation, I decided to use this newly learnt truth about feelings here! I took the firm decision to replace the old lies by the truth of God's love for me, whatever my feelings would say. I decided to chase away the lie by continually proclaiming the truth to my heart Rom.12:21), and by thanking the Lord for all His goodness and love, filling my thoughts with that, even though I "felt" to the contrary:- the lie. This I did for many days (!), under all daily tasks, to feed myself with the truth and to resist the lie. That way, unconsciously, I discovered an important principle: that you can speak to your soul, like David did (Psalm 42:5,11; 43:5). We can do this by continuing to proclaim the truth, like:

> "Isn't it wonderful that God is good, that He loves me, and that He is always with me!"

It is also very powerful to look for a Scripture verse that fits your own situation, and to base your proclamation on the Word of God. Doing this is not too hard for anyone; we only need to do this from a desire to obey the truth - and it works! In my life, it took some six weeks until I noticed that also my feelings started to change - I could grasp something of God's love for me. So do not give up: the result is more than worth it and it had a lasting effect on my life. Our thoughts and feelings may have been sickened by the lies of the enemy, but can be bathed clean in the "truth laundry" of God's Word, as we ask His forgiveness for letting the lies have their way with us. And what a consolation, that this truth (of a Father in heaven who is love) is so beautiful!

Receiving a loving God

In a later period in my life I noticed, even though I had received Christ at conversion (a life-changing event!), and even though later on I had received the Holy Spirit and His power in my life (Ac.1:8), that I had *never consciously received God the Father* in His eternal might in my heart, to have full sway there (Prov.23:26; Lk.10:27; Jhn.16:27; Rom.8:14-17). What a risky venture that seemed! This was the test. Was He really love? Did I truly believe He was love? I opened my heart to Him - and what a peace and dimension He has brought. True, it is an ongoing lesson to learn more about His love; but the more we open our hearts to Him, the more we experience that we do not need to expect things from people when the almighty God has made room in our life. Did you ever accept Him? Jesus gave His life to open up the way to the Father for us. Receiving the Father, therefore, must be of ultimate importance...

5.4 Avoiding "false humility" and passivity

Just like in Chapter 4 on insecurity, our lack of self-esteem can make us prone to sway between pride and (an often false) humility. We feel we are nothing, so others should not think they would be something... for that hurts our own lack of self-esteem! However, a solution can be found. Often, false humility may also stem from one of the following causes:

A. *The "I will never amount to much" thoughts* are a lie from the enemy. We have seen above how to deal with lies (Ch.5(3)): we consciously replace these with the truth. If we start believing such lies we hurt God who has created us with talents and abilities, because we then become prone not to use these God-given talents and bury them in the ground (Lk.19:12-16). This can also result from discouragement or from the negative opinions and jealousy of other people in our lives. It can even be proud to believe we have little value, because then we think we know better than God who created us and saw that it was "very good" (Gen.1:31). However, God does understand and He wants to encourage us! He is that kind of a God. The best medicine for this is: Writing down your strong points and abilities that He has given you (as in Ch.6 on identity). Thank Him often for these, and keep asking Him how you may put these personal qualities to good use for Him in any given situation. It can help to ask Him forgiveness about our passivity, if we feel we have not done things we should have. We can also ask Him for ideas on how to put our abilities to good use; a try-out in low-key church work or a hobby can be a "safe" start if we still feel insecure. Our Creator understands this so well, and wants you and me to have much space for creativity!

B. Some may fear, *"People should not think I am haughty"* by daring to step out and do certain things for God. That way, the fear of people's opinions can make us servile, a pride-in-disguise that does not want to show our true self. Much humility is needed to show some so-called pride, and simply daring to be ourselves is the very best medicine. It helps us to remember, that when we have not seen our own value, we might quite heavily underestimate Gods creation in us... We cannot be truly proud of ourselves - we received everything from Him (1.Cor.4:7) - but we may be proud of what He created and redeemed in us, and give Him the glory by letting our light shine before men fully (see Mt.5:16). This is a mission in life that we *all* have.

Therefore, let's not suppress our pride by "acting" humbly, but learn to give God the glory in everything we do (Col.3:17) - then, there will hardly be any room left for pride. True humility looks for the truth, listens to God, and lets itself be guided by Him; such humility is not a flight, is not the *absence* of pride, but the *presence* of courage: to show who we really are, to open our visor, daring to be vulnerable and to show our weaknesses. For only then will we be ready to also show and develop our gifts and abilities, in spite of any fear that the world might see how "proud" we are! That is a way in which we become like the seed that falls into earth and dies (Jhn.12:24-25), so that the Holy Spirit can bring forth His fruit in our life (Gal.5:22-23). Frequently, the problem is that we first of all want to be well-thought of by people around us, rather than by the Lord (Jhn.5:44) who judges things so differently and wants us to step up to a higher level of faith and maturity.

C. *Some may be afraid of "sticking their neck out"* and take risks, of making mistakes or of being noticed by others. However, this is the only way to make progress, as we can learn from the turtle... Developing our unique gifts will make us stand out among others as different, and it might sometimes even cause negative remarks or jealousy. For many of us this can be a bit scary, and we try to make ourselves obscure by going along with the crowd or even by withdrawing from them. That way, it will be hard to fulfill the God-given calling for our life, even when we have not fully discovered it yet! Much courage is needed to show our uniquely different personality: in our talents, our own opinion, and when necessary even in a confrontation with others who do wrong. We need to learn to take certain steps, and that can be hard at first. Chapter 3 on the fear of man may be of help in this.

Also, it may be a source of strength to thank the Father again and again for loving you so intensely, even when you feel you have no gifts or talents at all; that you are precious in His sight just the way He created you (Ps.139:13-14). Especially when you are not "feeling" this yet, it helps to keep remembering this truth. God accepts and notices us, not for all we have performed for Him, but for who we are and because of our loving relationship with Him. It makes Him enjoy you and me every day, and you may start experiencing this to your surprise!

5.5 Holding on to the objective truth regarding our own life

God, our Creator, is so tremendously good. He created us to His glory. He wants to heal us and build us up, to make something beautiful out of our lives. In what way have you been thinking about yourself so far? What do you believe about yourself? How do you speak about yourself? Many of us think and speak about ourselves in a negative way; but if we know that our sins have been forgiven, we are clean and beautiful in God's sight; our low self-esteem is then founded on a lie. Then, any negative attitude we have about ourselves has far-reaching consequences! Some of these appear below.

A. What are we influenced by?

Our negative thoughts and speech about ourselves (self-talk) influences our behavior, our attitude, and in the long run how we feel about ourselves. Our feelings of inferiority can have deep roots, to the measure that the events causing these had a deeper influence on our life, and to the measure that we allowed the resulting negative thoughts about ourselves any space in our heart. However, from my own experience I found that the way back is much the same:

(a) *Start to see those past events* (write down the ones that played a role in causing your negative thoughts and feelings) *in the loving light of God*, not in the light of difficult situations and people who have hurt us. For in all this, the heavenly Father stood right next to us, even if we did not know Him very well. So often, we failed to see His loving and outstretched hand to us while our eyes were fixed on our needs. By acknowledging this truth even in old difficult situations of the past, we can begin to see that even back then He loved and accepted us, that He wanted to be our refuge and strength (Ps.46). It is important to pray through such situations in this light and receive His consolation for these. It helps us if we forgive others who have failed and hurt us for the guilt they may have towards us, for their negative words and deeds. That way, old grudges and bitterness will no longer find room in us, and we get a foundation for the healing of our feelings. "Keep your wounds clean", someone once said. How true ... healing will then be promoted, rather then the wound getting infected more and more!

(b) *We can change our negative thoughts about ourselves* by a firm decision of our will to think more lovingly about ourselves and our abilities, and to stop allowing those negative thoughts to have any room - even though our old hurting feelings scream the opposite! (Ch.9(4)) It may help to write down what thus far you have thought and felt about yourself; then write down what God in His Word thinks about you (Is.43:4; Ps.146; Jdg.6:12-16; Deut.7:7-9). Then, replace those untrue thoughts by the truth of God's love (Ch.5(3)). Believe Him, obey Him from now on by being guided by His truth, not by negative and hurt feelings. It may help to learn some Bible verses by heart that you find helpful for your situation. Repeat them, fill your heart and thoughts with their truth, and stop being bothered with those old lies about you. They tear you down, a waste of your time and energy.

In this, we need not deny those less wonderful circumstances, habits and sins that in all objectivity may still be there in our life. For it is the truth that will set us free! We can bring all these needs to God, asking for His forgiveness, also forgiving others and even ourselves. Denying the truth will not help us at all. Some people may believe that by "positive thinking" they can manipulate circumstances or even get healed of an illness (by denying its existence and acting as if it were not there), or that by such thinking they can gather riches and honor. We will consciously avoid such a trap. God's truth and love have a healing effect on our souls, even when we have no health or riches.

(c) *Never speak negatively about yourself again*, unless it is the objective truth in God's sight (for instance, if you struggle with a weakness, or if you have sinned and need to ask forgiveness from someone). This is a serious matter; it tells your feelings that you are no good indeed. At one time, I learned deep lessons here in my own life. I worked for a fine Christian man, and as I made a typing error I called myself "stupid - however could I do that!" This man then walked to me, looked me very strictly in the eye and said: "I want to never ever hear that from you again. You are precious in God's sight!" I was thoroughly shaken by his unexpected strictness, and only later understood how deep the truth was that God had created me and "saw that it was very good" (Gen.1:31). That was the truth I had to hold on to, and - more than anything else - it helped to rebuild my life. How often do we say, "I wouldn't manage that", "I will mess this up anyway". With such unbelief, we will not only destroy your self-esteem, but (like I used to do) also harvest in our feelings and even our environment what negativity we have sown about ourselves. We may then even start measuring others with the same negative rod, thinking they must be just as "faulty" as we are. People around us will feel our negative expectations, and by these we can hinder them from blossoming in the talents God has given them. Therefore, we can see that thinking Gods beautiful thoughts about ourselves will also help us to expect beautiful things in others. Even when they sin, we know that God can restore them - we know it from our own experience!

It may also help us to start thanking God for what He created in us. "Thank you, Lord, that I am a boy/girl; thank you Lord for creating me, and creating me well; thank you that I can sing, or draw, or be a true friend to others, etc.

We can practice seeing what good things God has created in us, and speaking them out even to others. Take courage... everyone can learn this!

(d) *Choose to truly love yourself.* The God who Himself created us has done it so marvelously, and if we allow Him He keeps polishing us up joyfully! If we think otherwise, we make our loving Friend a liar... As long as we allow untrue negative thoughts about ourselves, we will find it difficult to love ourselves - no wonder. But when we start to accept how very uniquely God has made us, how even bad circumstances of the past will work for good to all who love God (Rom.8:28), well, then it is no longer so hard to realize that you are special! So - choose His truth about you, and start loving yourself by repeatedly choosing to do so. Choose His loving opinion, especially when your own wounded feelings don't really seem to grasp that truth: that you are loved, because of what Jesus has done for you. He loved you so much that He even died for you, to present you before the throne of grace! (Col.1:22; Jud.24; Rom.3:22-25; 2.Cor.4:14-18) Our feelings of unworthiness, our lack of self-esteem, can be healed if we hold on to the truth of God and start esteeming ourselves as worthy and lovable, just as God has esteemed us worthy of His love. Hold on to it, whatever your feelings say!

And the wonderful thing is, that the more we choose to accept the truth, consciously starting to respect, appreciate and forgive ourselves, the easier it becomes to also love, appreciate and forgive others! Other people notice it when you respect them. That way, our attitude towards ourselves helps us to be "transformed in our mind" (Rom.12:2) - how important... The respect that you learn to have for yourself as a child of God can even remain when you have sinned - not by having respect for the sin, but as we confess it and ask forgiveness before God (and where necessary before man), we can be cleansed of sin so that the "new creation" we are in Christ becomes manifest more and more (2.Cor.5:16-17).

B. *How can we get rid of lies?* This is very important - for with these the enemy can keep a foot between the door of our heart to get in with thoughts like, "nobody loves me", "I will never amount to anything", "I am really unlovable" - thoughts that can lead us to gloom and low self-esteem. Stop! It is *not* true. Allow no one to suggest that to you - not the enemy, not people, not circumstances, not experiences from the past, and especially not your own thinking. Don't be your own worst enemy... Feelings are deeply influenced by our thought life (Ch.5(3)), so let's guard the thoughts of our heart (Prov.4:23; Ps.19:14), and give the truth of the Bible the first place in our thoughts, up and against the "old feelings". What we sow in our thoughts, we will reap in our feelings and, finally, in our personality. As in the past we often failed to think according to God's truth, our feelings can have become a very unreliable measure, like a deformed yardstick. They can be healed as we bring our thinking in line with the truth of God's love and of His Word. Read especially about how positively God thinks of us! (2.Cor.3:18; Col.3:10; Rom.8:29-39; Eph.1:3-14; 1.Joh.3:1-3). The way we treat ourselves shows which way we treat Gods creation in us - let's make sure we start honoring God for it!

Have you already learned to appreciate the good and beautiful things in yourself? (Even make a list - asking others to help if you cannot come up with much yet.) Have you already decided to love yourself, or are you still measuring yourself by the crooked yardstick of your feelings? Then you might miss seeing some of the valuable things that God has for you - wouldn't that be a pity... Therefore, it is important to thank the Lord frequently for your life, and to read of the many encouragements that can give us a new perspective as Christians (e.g. in Ephesians and Colossians).

5.6 Paying attention to our appearance

We can glorify God even with our appearance and show how beautiful His creation is - not for vanity, or to cover up our insecurity, or to make others jealous; but to give Him the glory for who He has made us. This is an attitude we can ask Him for. We may feel that we are not beautiful or rich at all. But if we are neatly dressed in colors that suit us; clean and well-groomed, we can be more pleasant to be with. It will help us in our testimony and contacts with others if we look right and do the best we can; it will also help our self-esteem.

It is important to ask ourselves, "What is it really that *I myself* find beautiful?" "What can bring out the special things God has given me?" "What would please God?" His Word speaks of us as a royal priesthood, clothed in spotless, white garments - a sign that our inner being is in harmony with Him, that our sins have been forgiven (Rev.19:8; Jhn.19:23-24; Is.61:3; Ex.28:2-6; Lev.16:4). We do not really need to dress in white outwardly, but if we have a relationship of love with Him, something of that will shine through to others - even if our clothes are not very new or fashionable. That inward cleanliness is not apparent through a showy display of our new clothes (1.Pet.3:3-4), but through an inner purity, simplicity and good taste. It is good to pay some attention to this in the way we dress (even spend some money), if we have a possibility to do so. With the right motives, we may use some make-up: "if the barn needs painting, paint it" - just be modest. Looking our best within the means we have will also help us to remain aware of our value as a person.

A lack of self-esteem can often show through our outward looks, and at this time of our life we may weapon ourselves against this. Not by being sloppily dressed - or even by being "overdressed" out of insecurity - but by looking right, by knowing that it is OK to be the person we are with the taste we have. It may be important to choose not so much "what people like" (peer pressure or vanity - we are already esteemed by God) but to choose what *we* would really like, and what glorifies God. He knows our immense worth, and we may truly be seen as His creation. Personally, I have really had to learn this.

Let me tell you of a handicapped friend of mine. Her face has been deformed since childhood, she is very fat indeed, she has no good taste and she knows it. To make up for it, she regularly goes to the hairdresser, and once or twice a year goes to a fashion shop where the sales ladies know her - and give good advice on what dresses to buy. In church, she looks at her "Sunday's best". She is a gifted person, she loves the Lord wholeheartedly, and He uses her - and people love her! She rents a hotel lobby for her birthdays...

Perhaps you will think, "but I'm not even interested in clothes" - yet even then, you will be a good testimony for the Lord to look at least neat and well-groomed, however limited your wardrobe is. You can ask someone with a good taste to help when you buy something. Just look for good quality, easy maintenance, and a color that looks good on you. May not our outward looks confirm what we used to think inwardly: "I will never amount to anything". *It is not true!*

5.7 Do not look down on your task and position

It is not our task in life that will give us an esteemed position, but as children of the king (a position we already have!) we may make even the lowliest task into something we can do to the glory of God; we "make something out of it" by doing it unto the Lord personally and under His commission. He sees what no one else will ever see, and it will gladden His heart when we glorify Him. May the quality of our work be worthy of the King! We may put all of our abilities, creativity, dedication and love in our daily work, as something we can present to Him. That way, we honor Him (not ourselves) before others around us who know that we are Christians, as a good testimony. Especially in those things that we do not really like doing, God knows that we bring a sacrifice - it is a gift that brings joy to His heart! Therefore, give the best you have, irrespective of personal financial gains.

It is in simple tasks that God can prepare us for a more difficult one (Mt.25:23). That way, we can grow in faithfulness and in learning to do the daily chores to the glory of God - especially in tasks where there is little honor to be gained for ourselves. From my own life, I can testify that by doing tasks nobody else liked, and putting some of my creativity and joy in it for the Lord, I would start liking such a task, and in the end others believed that I had grasped that "nice job" for myself! Done with love, even simple tasks become honorable and are lifted to a higher level; they lose their ugliness both in our eyes and the eyes of others. Also, this is a good training for our character, a situation in which we learn to love the Lord in practice, to be faithful, to be a good testimony for Him through our work, as well as an opportunity to bless others in our daily duties.

A living example to me was an elderly American pastor, who told us of the small churches where he had served. He always seemed to be the one who had to clean the toilets. But he experienced then that especially the lowly positions can be God's true place of anointing. He told us of David, called by God, who nevertheless had to flee to Adullam, where a bunch of other outcasts joined him (1.Sam.22:1-2). Where was God's promise? Saul despised him; yet that difficult time, without any position and with so many problems, was the time of God's true preparation for David's royal office. There he learned to remain faithful to God, and what it meant to be a true leader.

Therefore, let us not be jealous of the jobs and positions of others. Every job knows its (sometimes big) problems and less nice tasks. The secret is the love relationship of our heart with Jesus. Real joy, fruitfulness, and promotion come from the heart of God, however little other people may esteem us.

5.8 Learning to show appreciation to others

By being rich in our relationship with Jesus, we can become freer and less self-focused; by becoming open to Him we can also become more open to others. By learning to appreciate ourselves, it also becomes easier to see the value of others and how beautifully God has made them - and we can become more sensitive to the beauty of His creation. God has put *His own worth* in them when He created them, and made them truly "worthwhile". We can find out whatever is good in them, and start appreciating them for who they are, not only for what they do. They may not be perfect yet! We can look for the beautiful things the Creator has put in them, their special personality in which He wants to reveal Himself. It helps to encourage them. What can we see of Gods design in the other person? This will give us faith for their future. Prov.11:25 is encouraging. As we start appreciating others, we may also learn afresh to appreciate what beauty He has given to us!

So, let's give each other the space to be ourselves and to blossom for the Lord, letting the other person feel that they are of deep worth to God and to others, without flattering them. Have you given anyone a true compliment this past week or month yet? Even some children do not receive enough encouragement, and it can affect their adult life. As we may know from experience how important it is to be appreciated and encouraged, let us try to do that for others as well!

6
IN SEARCH OF OUR IDENTITY

Many of us wrestle with the question, "Who am I?", and have not fully made the tremendous discovery of who God has created us to be, and what He gave to us in our personality and talents. We do not need to try getting an identity; we already have one. The Creator has made us and saw that it was "very good"! (Gen.1:31; Ps.139:14-16) He created a treasure box inside of us and, if we did not like who we are, this treasure box may never have been opened to the full.

The following thoughts may be of help on this treasure hunt!

6.1 Asking our Master

The God Who created us is the only One who fully knows our identity and purpose. He has the answer. Often, we ourselves try to find out who we are: from events in life, through whatever makes us different from others, through experiences in our contacts with people (which may not always be happy ones), or by what we think of our own abilities. We believe that this is "who we are". However, that is at best just part of the truth! It is not what others or we ourselves think, it is not what the enemy whispers in negativity, it is not who we seem to be through hurtful experiences of the past - but only what God has created in us that makes up who we really are. His thoughts often are quite different from ours - they are much higher and more beautiful! (Is.55:8-9; Jer.29:11)

Quite a few people try to build up their own identity; they work on improving their "self-image". What they really are doing is trying to look better in the eyes of other people!

They may not try to truly become better people in a desire to obey God or to discover His will for their life - a will that is always in line with their talents and personality. By working on improving their own self-image - it may sound strange - such people may even lose sight of their God-given identity, of what God has created them for! They want to make something out of themselves, to seem different and better than they really are. They want to make a "name for themselves" like at the tower of Babel. (Gen.11:4; John 5:44), seeking their own glory, polishing themselves up, wanting to be like someone else. However, discovering the image God created in us (Gen.1:26) is *finding our true self-image*. Only as I started to really discover what God created in me, did I learn to appreciate and use my own gifts, and recognize and appreciate my own personality that differed from that of all the others! Only then did I "dare to be myself" and, finally, was able to thank Him for who He made me - knowing that His steady hand would guide me.

God has His own purpose for our life, and He wants us to discover how beautifully He created us. If we disregard that or do not really appreciate it, we overlook what is most essential about us. We have received *one* identity only, and if we push away Gods building blocks for our life, we can only build dream castles that cannot become true. Just start discovering in what respects God has made you special! If you want God to build you up, start with the solid foundation for your life: making sure that your sins have been forgiven, so that the building of your life will stand firmly upon the rock that is Christ. When our sins have been washed away, and the dust has been rinsed off our building blocks, we may also see more clearly the blueprint for our life and the contours of Gods work of art inside us - the essence of our being!

6.2 Using our instrument

Take a good look at your hand; open and close your fingers. What a gift, what possibilities! God made us beautiful instruments with which, in the hand of the Master, beautiful things can be done. All that God has created in us is like an instrument that we may learn to use for His Kingdom; and the way we are to use it depends on the kind of instrument! We can learn to manage our gifts responsibly. It is like with every instrument: we can decide to use it for good or for bad purposes... if we allow the enemy to use us, bad things will happen. The question is: for which master do we choose to work? (Rom.6:12-23; Mt.6:24) For whom, and by whom, do we let ourselves be used? Even the best instrument can cause terrible damage when in the wrong hands; yet even the frailest instrument, in the hands of the Master and guided by the Holy Spirit, can serve a beautiful goal! (Eph.2:10, 4:23-24; Col.1:10-16, 3:10; Rom.6:4-13). A few examples of the use of our talents:

Guided by God's Spirit:	Guided by the enemy:
endurance	stubbornness
sensitivity	touchiness
wisdom	slyness
tact, discreetness	manipulation
ability to obey God	slavish attitude

We could think of many such examples, but the idea is clear: once we yield ourselves (i.e. the instrument that we are) to righteousness, placing it under the control of God's Holy Spirit, our life will change totally. The instrument is the same, but now it is used by Him Who fashioned it and knows it intimately. God knows what He can do with it, and how to chisel a work of art from our material, slowly but surely.

The "old man" belongs to the sinful category - "self" is on the throne (taking the place of worship in our heart), or perhaps "self" has given up hope ("nobody wants me anyway"). Still, the solution is clear: Placed in the hands of God, even our deformed and negative character twists can be put right, cleansed and healed, for the beautiful purpose God has in store for us! So let's place our life and talents into God's hands, let them function in obedience to Him - on the basis of the forgiveness of our sins, not because we "deserve" anything. From then on, we will be able to overcome evil with good (Rom.12:20-21). It really is the only way...

We cannot keep hiding from the bad things we do and, in our weakness, even fighting these may have little effect. The only way to break free from this is: to ask God to forgive us whenever we sinned (our redemption is in this). (Col.1:13-14) We can then place our lives afresh into the hands of God, under the guidance of the Holy Spirit and pray once again for the infilling with His power. Thus, we direct ourselves again towards the good, acceptable and perfect will of God for our life (Rom.12:1-2; Hebr.13:20-21).

Knowing this may also help us to build up others, for instance where in the past we tended to slander, we now start elevating the good qualities of others; this is something we can learn to do in all of our conversations. Then, we will build up instead of tearing others down. It is good to remember the "golden rule" (Mt.7:12) that, as we would want others to treat us, we ourselves should treat them - even though they are not perfect yet! If they really do sin, go to them in private rather than telling others about it (Mt.18:15-17); and remember to forgive... That is more difficult but the right way.

The way we handle our relationships is very important to God. It's better to be constructive, not focusing on the evil around you but on promoting what is good. If we occupy ourselves with that, we will soon have little time or attention left for slander. Do we seek for what is good? May Philippians 4:8 become one of our favorite Scripture verses; it has such beautiful things to say.

6.3 A child of the King

For God it is more important *who* we are than *what* we are. God created us to have friendship - a love relationship - with Him, not to let us produce many good works. We know that the way of salvation is by grace and not by good works, yet so many of us act as if that were so. The world in its economy wants as much production as possible; yet for

God it is important that we love Jesus and take time with Him – far more important than any ministry for Him. Even though He has given us different gifts and talents, these are not the most important things He wants us to focus on. Our personal contact with Him is of the uttermost importance! More than that: He Himself lives in us; we can give Him more and more room in our weak hearts so that it becomes His throne room. The more we become acquainted with Him, the more we dare to be ourselves with Him. He is with us in all situations, and we can tell Him everything that moves our hearts. We may try to solve problems by our many efforts, but if instead we seek His face and throw ourselves in His arms, He can do things through us that we ourselves could never have done. (Php.4:13; Eph.3:16-20; Col.1:11-12) His eyes can guide us when we keep looking up at Him. He is our Goal, our Guidance.

However talented we may be, only those things that have been initiated by Him in our life will have eternal value and will remain. We can all learn to listen to Him, as we ask: "What do You want me to do? Which way am I to go?" From the Bible, much is already clear. Yet for specific situations, as we seek new direction in life, we need to especially feel His guiding hand.

In Youth with a Mission, they teach an important principle for guidance:

Ask God what He wants you to do;
Wait until He speaks;
Do what He tells you to.

It sounds so simple, but it can be so hard to wait on God! It's very important that we learn to listen (1.Sam.3:10b).

Firstly, we see that we are to find our strength in the Lord and in our relationship with Him, rather than leaning on our talents. He must be the Author and Finisher of our actions, so that we can have faith in what we do. If we look at Him first, He can change us, and the beautiful things He has put inside of us can come to fruition in the right situations. (2.Cor.3:18; 5:17; Mt.6:33-34; Gal.5:22-23)

Secondly, it is helpful to read of *God's truth about you* in the Bible. What are God's thoughts about *me*? Just a small selection of these:
- God created me as a precious human being; He is proud of me and encourages me; I am pleasing Him because He loves me, and not because of what I do for Him to deserve anything. (Is.43:1-7; Ps.139:13-14; Deut.7:7-9)
- God already loved me while I was a sinner. (Rom.5:8; 1.Cor.1:27-31; Lk.5:32; 1.Jhn.4:10)
- Angels rejoiced when I as a sinner turned to Him for salvation. (Luk.15:7,10)
- He forgave my sins; now I am a new creation, clean and holy before Him. (Therefore, it is so important to make sure that we bring our sins daily before Him and receive His forgiveness and cleansing!) (1.Jhn.1:8-9; 1.Cor.6:11; 2.Cor.5:17; Eph.2:1-10)
- He drew me out of darkness and placed me into the Kingdom of His dear Son. (Col.1:13-14; Eph.5:8; Tit.3:3-7; Mt.25:34-40)
- I am a child of the King and belong to His royal priesthood. (Jhn.1:12; 1.Pet.2:9-10)
- God is my heavenly Father and will never leave me; He is always beside me. (Ps.16:8; Is.49:15-16; Jhn.10:28-29; Rom.8:35)
- I am more than a conqueror through our Lord Jesus Christ. (Rom.8:37; 1.Cor.15:57; Rev.15:1-3)

6.4 God's special blueprint

Be deeply convinced that God has unique plans for you. God created you with special talents in line with the goals that He has for *your* life. In many cases we have not even taken the trouble to discover these!

God's goodness is embodied in His plans with us. He will not give us a task that we cannot fulfill. He created us with the abilities and talents that match with the place and task that He has in store for us, and that we may even come to enjoy

(Ps.40:8)! On top of that, He gives us spiritual gifts to help us fulfill His task (1.Cor.12:1-11; 14:1-12) and to edify His church. As we keep following Him and opening ourselves up to the work of the Holy Spirit (asking Him for more of His power), His fruit can grow: love, joy, peace,... (Gal.5:22-23). Also, let us not forget that whatever we lack in abilities or spiritual gifts, He can fulfill by people who stand next to us, by new circumstances, and by His special guidance in our life. We cannot do the task alone; we need Him, and we need others who are also guided by Him.

To some of us, it may seem hard to imagine that God's will for our life can make us happy! However, we can recognize His voice as coming from the Good Shepherd, with all the qualities of the fruit of the Holy Spirit (Gal.5:22-23). This is Who God is and what His guiding voice is like. He is concerned about our welfare, trying to get us from wrong ways onto His right way (Jer.29:11-14). This does not mean that we will not see times of trouble in this fallen world, but He does give a song into our heart when we keep walking in His way.

Therefore, let us not simply copy other people whom God guides differently and for whom He may have somewhat different goals. God wants to guide you along His special path for you - fitting in with the way He made you like no one else! The task He has for you will be fulfilled even more if you are filled with His thoughts (reading in the Bible) and live close to Him. *Our thoughts are the strongest influence in the direction that we go* (see also Ch.9)! It is important that we start thinking about ourselves the way God sees us: as precious and irreplaceable people in God's Kingdom, for whom He has a holy and unique destiny that other people may not be able to see. Have you asked Him yet about the goals and calling for your life? If you have never done so, a great challenge lies ahead: to start discovering the beautiful purpose that God has in store specifically for you.

It is not true that others have received everything and you have been given nothing. If you are objectively honest, then you will know that you, too, have been given special gifts and opportunities - only different, in line with your personality and calling. The gifts of others would not necessarily match with who you are! People who seem less talented and less well-educated, but who use their talents faithfully and with dedication, may often achieve more than the very talented who spend less time and dedication on using their gifts. Every talent is special, but we must want to see that. We have lived all our life with our own talents and may not realize just how special they are, not even that they are talents at all. Many of us have not buried our talents (Mt.25:14-28) but never truly realized we had them. God knows, and He wants to use these in a hurting world!

Therefore, it is important that we start appreciating what God has given us - even if we were not truly impressed with ourselves before! Let's make the very most of it, to His glory. Do not let the enemy with his negativity take this away from you any longer, but start looking with new eyes at yourself and your talents that you have regarded as "so ordinary" in the past... Ch. 5 on self-worth may also be of help.

6.5 Being unique means being different

As we discover the aspects in which God has created us uniquely, we will notice how we differ from others. No matter how we look at it, we *are* unique and different. It will not help us to try hiding in the crowd... We have a separate identity - perhaps a shock, but certainly a challenge! Perhaps He has already spoken to you about your identity and calling in the past - through promises in His Word, encouragements by others, etc. These are very important pieces of information.

The example of the teaspoon

We may discover more about our identity by looking at ourselves intently. Let me give you an example. If we were to pick up a teaspoon, and came from a totally different culture without such utensils (say, the Stone Age), we would try to describe what it is and what it is intended for. How? Perhaps by noticing: "It is long, made of some sort of metal, with on one side an oval hollow part. It clearly has been made for some specific use, and it has an elegant form. Perhaps I could use it as a scoop, or stir something with it." How did we describe the teaspoon? How do we try to find out what it could be used for? – right: by noticing what characteristics, form and qualities this instrument *does* have, not by describing all that it is *not*! It would be hard to discover its use, if we only describe what it is not: "It is not square, it is not fluid, not made out of stone; we cannot write with it...". That way it would take others a long time to find out what this thing even looked like! It is true, the teaspoon is not good for writing, and yet it is so useful that we don't want to be without it.

However, we sometimes act just like that when it comes to describing ourselves! We cannot find out who we are by summing up what we are not: "What am I even good for; I am not like Albert Einstein or Mother Theresa, I never won a contest, my French is awful, my chances for promotion are minimal, and I am not half as good at soccer as Jim...". Rather, let's find out what we *do* have! What instrument are *we*? You can learn from this not to look at the gifts of others, but at what God in His wisdom has given to *you* specifically; things you have become so used to that you fail to regard them as special - things, therefore, that you have to rediscover. How?

A. Buy an attractive notebook and make a list of:
- Your talents and specialties (things you know or can do).
- Your hobbies and things you like doing (or used to like as a child).
- Things that you find easy to do.
- Qualities that other people have noticed in you.
- Things you would enjoy doing for the Lord, not just in Church but also elsewhere.
- Any compliments that you have received.
- The topics in school that you liked best or that you got good notes for.
- The qualities in your personality (like readiness to help, honesty, understanding, an ability to listen, enthusiasm, or whatever it may be).

- Your dreams and ideals.
- Your physically strong points (abilities, endurance, nice hair, etc.).
- The talents and good things in our parents or even grandparents - we mostly inherited something beautiful or good from them that we can add to our list (this can also help us to get a fresh and positive look at our parents...).
- Anything our relatives and good friends tell us as we ask them about our good points. If they also see weak points, we can pray for improvement; yet here we need to remember that presently we are not looking for what is *not* there but for what *is* (in our search for who we are, not for what we are not, in our identity).
- Finally, God wants to also endow us with the power of the Holy Spirit and with the "spiritual gifts" we need in order to be fully equipped for the tasks He has for us. We can pray for these (Rom.12:4-8; 1.Cor.12:4-20; 14:1) and, if necessary, read some good books about it.

It is important that we keep adding to this list anything new we discover, especially if our list is still short. Keep the notebook at hand, ready to include anything new. *This is great fun...*

B. *Looking intently at the above list, thank the Lord* for the qualities that He has given to you, asking Him how you may develop these. Our life is an instrument for a specific task (just like the teaspoon!), and as we start making better use of our abilities, we will discover more possibilities that are dormant in us. Our gifts can develop as we start using them more! As we look at our list and put several abilities together, we may see some new combinations that give our talents a new scope. As you prayerfully engage in this search, you may see a pattern and perspective for your talents, personality, and even your life emerge. It will also help us discover how special we are. God has invested in us from the start (Ps.139:13-18). We can ask Him for His priorities, for things we can do for and with Him at this moment or in the future, and write these carefully into our notebook.

C. We may *ask the Lord for practical opportunities* to use those beautiful gifts and talents as best we can for His glory and kingdom (Mt.5:16; Rom.11:36). It helps to pray about this a lot. It has been His desire from the start to bring out what He has created in us and to let it blossom. There is really no one on earth with the exact same gifts, experiences, backgrounds, and personality that you have. They may look insignificant and over-familiar in our own eyes, but they are not! Dig up that hidden treasure, unwrap it as His gift to you. Let not the enemy in his disdain render yet another instrument in God's kingdom ineffective, but make the best of your talents and time.

6.6 Asking God for a tangible goal, a dream, or an ideal.

We all need something that is worth praying, striving, and working for; something we can be enthusiastic about and direct our energy towards - something constructive by which we can be used of God to help build His kingdom on earth. This will be something that fits our talents and personality. It helps to also write such things down: What were the things (however small) we used to dream of years ago? What ideals did we have more recently? It can be good to ask God if these contain some of His goals for our life. We can also ask God to give us His goals (and even ideals). In the end, He Himself is our goal - He determines the plan for our life as well as the smaller goals in between. In the beginning, such goals can be very simple, whereas later on they may grow and become visible to the outside world. Yet whatever is done out of love to Him, will be quite important in the sight of God.

If God is the origin and inspiration of our ideals, and if we have received a goal from Him, we may rest assured that He will also take care of the results if we follow Him and remain close to Him (Jhn.15:4-5) - for the plan came from Him and we had asked Him for it. By doing working on these, we may learn to see the greater picture of what He is calling us for. People who had the courage to dram have often reached remarkable things in history...

A good starting point will always be to pray for the details of our daily work. In these daily chores, God can prepare us for the future. Even in a simple job we can glorify God by investing something extra in it - in faithfulness, love, honesty, and also with our creative gifts if we find some room to exercise these. It may also be our testimony before others who may not respond to our words, for our lifestyle can speak louder than these. (Mt.5:16) We can ask God how to try out and test our qualities in everyday life and to teach us how to get along with other people. In Gods Kingdom, that is always so important!

As He guides and leads us, the Lord may ask us to focus especially on a specific area of our talents or to do some extra training - even if we often cannot see the further goal for our life. The way often goes step by step, and He wants us to be prayerfully connected to Him with each new step, to keep us in His will and on the small and narrow way. Now and then, God may show us a new part of the way ahead or give us a promise from His Word - and that is something very precious, like a compass by which we can redirect our life. Again, it helps us to write these important things down (with a date) and to hold on to them.

As in all details of life, it is important to pray for wisdom and for the strength of the Holy Spirit, who guides us into all truth (Jhn.14:17; 16:13). If He indeed calls us for a certain task, He will also give us the certainty, the courage, and the funds. His calling is more important than whether or not we have already discovered our specific talents. He has chosen to use weak people who ask for His forgiveness when they sin, wanting to remain close to Him. Therefore, let us not despise our dreams and ideals, but pray about these to discover God's will - and in what way He wants to use us. Focusing on God's goals also helps us to not look back to the fruitlessness or impossibilities of the past, but to constructively be engaged with God's possibilities for the future.

6.7 Encouraging others in their identity

When we start discovering more of the beautiful things God has placed inside of us, we will also see those more easily in other people. It also works the other way around: if we can appreciate how special the other person is, we will also more easily appreciate our own qualities. As we give to others (especially the ones that do not think very highly of themselves and do not yet fully blossom) our personal attention and respect whenever we can, we may also grow in insight about what God has entrusted to them - even if they themselves have not quite discovered this yet. They, too, are people who are irreplaceable and precious in Gods Kingdom. He wants to give them the desires of their heart if they seek their joy in Him (Ps.37:4). It helps us to find out how such people think about themselves. Pray for them, and - if they are open to it - try to tell them what special talents God gave them.

We can pray and think much about what good characteristics and possibilities God has given to the other person, and how he or she could start to blossom personally and as a Christian; about where he or she can find an opportunity to develop these qualities. Give them the chances you would have wanted for yourself, if this stimulates their development and if the Lord guides you to do so (Is.58:10-11). In our selfish world, this is a good example and testimony, furthering His Kingdom. As we focus on the well-being of others, God quietly takes care of our own identity and well-being - as His servants.

7
FROM LONELINESS TO RELATIONSHIPS

As someone to whom good friendships did not simply "occur", and having known times of loneliness like so many, I would like to share with you what has helped me through the years with some of the thoughts below.

7.1 All of us feel lonely at times

It certainly is no disgrace to feel lonely, and most of us experience times in which we have little real contact with others. In the midst of such times we may realize that, however lonely we may *feel*, we never really *are* lonely - for the Lord is always there for us! Being by ourselves does not necessarily mean experiencing feelings of loneliness; yet it does happen to many of us, and it helps if we use these times to learn to lean upon God. We may realize that even "strong personalities" experience feelings of loneliness (perhaps even more than others would!) in which they do not feel understood and cannot easily give themselves to other people. Our Lord must, humanly speaking, have been very lonely - no one on earth fully understood Him; and especially on the cross, when even the Father seemed to take His eyes off Him (Mt.27:46), He must have been extremely lonely. He understands our feelings. He has carried even this cross for us, so that we would no longer need to be lonely. He is our most faithful Friend and our Advocate, interceding for us with the Father. He knows the pain of loneliness from experience and desires for us to have relationships - the Bible speaks so much about relationships! (Gen.2:18; Mt.22:37-39)

The Lord Jesus wants to teach and help us develop the best kind of relationships with others. Even if people fail us, He

Himself is with us (Ps.27:10). He has opened the way to the Heavenly Father for us; we can have an intimate relationship with Him, and He has given us the Holy Spirit as Comforter and to strengthen us (Jhn.14:17-18). If we have opened our hearts to Him, we are in very good company!

A. *Never look down upon yourself*, if at times you feel lonely or unappreciated. You may not be "in" with the crowd, but you *are* worthwhile! Your feelings may not say so, but God does (Ch.5.1; 6.2; 9). This is a good opportunity to start respecting yourself as a creation of God, as a child of the King! We need not be unduly influenced by the opinion of imperfect people around us, but can hold on to the opinion of our loving Heavenly Father who knows us inside out. His opinion of us is the truth, and we can feel safe in His love and forgiveness, however imperfect we are. We will be encouraged as we strengthen our relationship with God as our heavenly Father (Ch.5.3) and, by seeking Him often in prayer, we will also grow in maturity and become less dependent on the opinion of people around us or on circumstances. This is something we can keep choosing to do. It can be a battle, but it does bring victory – a battle which we can learn from deeply.

Once we start seeing our own value we will begin radiating this, and it becomes easier for those around us to see the good things in us too. However, if we do not appreciate ourselves, we keep holding on to the lie that we are not worthwhile, and - unintentionally - we could make it easier for others to believe the same lie about us. That is another reason why we need to embrace God's loving truth about us. He created us as special beings; we are precious in His sight, no matter who we are. (Jhn.3:15-17; Is.43:1-7)

B. *Realize that there is no real reason for discouragement*. Perhaps loneliness overwhelms us now and then, but we may resist it with the truth: our loving Lord is always standing next to us, as our eternally reliable Friend, and no one will be able to snatch us from His hand (Jhn.10:27-29; Mt.28:20). So take hold of this truth, and don't let the enemy mislead you with his lies: that nobody would stand next to you or love you. It is *not* true! Our loving Lord stands next to us and never leaves us. If we speak this to our soul again and again, this encouraging truth will start sinking into its deeper levels, and in the end even our emotions can receive comfort and healing (see Ch.5(3)). The Lord stands next to us whatever man may do to us - so we do not blame it on Him but we may throw ourselves on Him, pouring our heart out; He understands (Ps.62:5-8). Self-pity works destructively, so we may need to start counting our blessings rather than our misfortunes, and to direct our thoughts to more constructive things.

When times are difficult, the enemy may often try to get us entangled in feelings of misery. In such cases, we can focus our thoughts on the truth, in the safe knowledge that we are in God's comforting Presence. Therefore, we should treasure our relationship with Him. Whoever loves God will learn how to build a deeper relationship with Him, and from that also with others - for He has created us for relationships.

7.2 Feelings of rejection and loneliness

Most of us struggled at times with such feelings, which can make being alone a painful thing. The origin of such feelings often lies in difficult experiences in the past, especially when we were still children and unable to handle situations of loneliness. We cannot turn the past around, but God can heal us!

A. *Rejection in our youth.* We can ask the Lord to help us remember any situations of rejection in our early youth, when we were left alone, ridiculed, or not accepted. Pray about this, and ask the Lord to go back with you to such painful situations. Bring your feelings of pain to Him in prayer. Even then, He stood next to you with His love - however invisible - so ready to take your hand, even though you may not have known Him very well at that time. You can grasp His extended hand even now for help in that old situation! Realizing His deep love and compassion for you, even back then, can change your whole view of it. Tell Him that you accept Him as the God who stood next to you also then, whenever you remember that situation or experience a similar one. He knows you intimately and feels the pain with you. Take a good look at His love and thank Him for it, receiving His comfort.

As a very small child, during a brief vacation right after the Second World War, I went camping with my father in a meadow. Now he may not have thought of it, but towards the end of the war a plane had been shot down and fell into a meadow very close to our home - a terrifying experience. Meadows did not feel safe; they were a place of death to me. One night during this vacation, I woke up in our tent - alone! My daddy had gone! I went outside but there was no one - and I stood crying on that dark and lonely meadow - unprotected in the "place of death". He was probably making a walk or seeking company in a nearby café, thinking I was soundly asleep, but I was absolutely in panic. Although over the years I had almost forgotten this experience, I later on often wondered why being left alone by others could cause such a sharp pain that could not be soothed by anything. In such cases, I felt left out, rejected, unloved, and guilty - perhaps not worthy to live. All this was based on the conclusions of an immature child, too young to deal with that situation. Yet looking back on that night many years ago, I now know for a fact that Jesus was there. I also had to forgive my father (I could do that, once I realized the guilt was not mine). As a result, the pain decreased, and I no longer felt I had to hold on to people for fear of that recurring pain of desertion. Now that the true cause had emerged and I had asked God to work on it, those wrong childish responses could be healed. How? We can see more on that below.

B. *Forgive all the people involved in such situations from your heart.* Perhaps you will never find out if they were truly guilty, but your feelings were hurt and, therefore, it is good to firmly decide to forgive all of them fully. We can speak this out before God. The person may no longer be alive, but even then, an attitude of forgiveness is what we can speak out towards God. Let no bacteria of bitterness grow in the painful open wounds of our memory! Then, we may pray for God to deeply bless these people (if they are still alive) and ask if He will fill our memory of this event with His peace; for even back then He stood next to us in His love, however little we realized it.

C. *We also ask the Lord to forgive our own sins - be it in this event or as a result of it* - for instance: if we allowed the old pain to grow into any bitterness against people, affecting relationships with those around us, or if we easily mistrust others when similar situations occur. In such situations, we then have not acted from faith but out of the old hurts, and that can make us suspicious of others. We may believe the other person has bad motives that, in fact, they may not have at all (we can falsely accuse them in our hearts). It is good to detect on which kind of occasions this happens in our life, so that we may pinpoint when it started and deal with the real cause. Moreover, we can choose to think the best of the other person, should such a situation happen again. Our feelings may still "scream" for a while, whilst our mind already knows of the real and painful cause from the past. Let's be at rest, for we can - as it were - speak to our feelings about the truth (Ch.5(3)). The truth is: that there is a Heavenly Father who intensely loves us whatever we go through, that the Lord Jesus wants to be our Friend who will never leave us, and that our painful feelings are a reminder of some old wounds. Such wounds will heal faster, if we truly forgive those who were hurting us. The Bible even teaches us to be a blessing to them (Rom.12:14,20-21; 1.Cor.4:12-13).

7.3 Making special use of this time

We can use this time, when there are few deep relationships in our life, for a special purpose. Believe it or not, this can become a very precious time in our life, in which we allow God to deepen His relationship with us. Perhaps there will soon come a season in which we are far too busy - perhaps also by working in His Kingdom - to work on these things in the same measure! So let's not miss this "time to spare", but use the opportunity to the full. It may not return for a long time. During this time, your prayer life can reach a new intensity, the Bible can speak to you afresh, and your knowledge will increase. It worked that way in my own life. In my thirties, I came to work in a new town, and it took several years before I prayerfully found some true friends. However, in those years I learned how to cope with living on my own and leaning on the Lord, as well as using my time as best I could. Even today, I still lean on the Bible knowledge accumulated during those years.

A. *Take time to spend with the Lord, to be in "first love" with Him* (Rev.2:4). Perhaps you still hold on too much to the opinion or appreciation of others, or to your own goals and work? If so, now is a good time to be with the Lord Jesus and enjoy Him. If you do not yet know that "first love", then God so desires to work on that during this period, in which earthly friendships do not yet demand so much of your time and energy that at times they threaten our quality time with Him (App.1). His presence will refresh you and renew your vision, and can help you grow in maturity (Is.41:10; Ps.16:8-11). Our problems and impossibilities are often Gods opportunities.

B. *There are some real advantages in being "by yourself"*, especially for those who are unmarried and have no children to take care of. For them, God has a special calling, special opportunities, and many possibilities. Should you belong in this category, then use your freedom to go where God calls you, to do things for which others have less opportunity, and be encouraged by the special task God has for you (1.Cor.7:32-35). Perhaps not every church may recognize the unique role God has in store for single people, as those being set apart for Him, but God Himself is true to His Word (Jer.1:12). Therefore, use your opportunities to seek and serve Him, both for the development of your Christian character and for the furthering of His Kingdom. Even if you do not yet notice many improvements at this point, God gives special love and promises to the lonely (Ps.68:5-6; Ps.27).

C. *Spend your free time in a useful way*, constructively and creatively. This can be very important, for by the time you will have more friends and tasks, there may be little time left for hobbies or a course, and you may be very sorry later. What is it that you really want to do - learn a new skill, get involved in music or painting? Take a cookery course? In times like this, it is easy to hide behind professional activity, but it can do us a world of good to do things we really enjoy. It is a good medicine against being discouraged, while we are still in the process of learning wisdom and new things God wants to teach us by His Holy Spirit. Did you ever wonder what it is, that you would really enjoy doing? Sometimes, I was so bored by the repetition of daily duties that I had to consciously ask myself this question. It helps to make a little list of these things: What is it that I used to enjoy? What relaxes me? What speaks to my heart? We can consciously set aside some time to relax - a great walk in fine weather, do some nice work in the garden, or just visit a relative.

7.4 Helped by the Comforter

It helps us to keep praying for the fullness of the Holy Spirit as we do our daily tasks. The Holy Spirit is the Comforter that God has promised; from Him come wisdom, encouragement, confidence, power, and the fruit of the Spirit (Gal.5:22-23)! It will also help us ask for love towards people, to reach them and no longer focus on our own needs. Moreover, we can ask for His humility to reach those who are not honoured by the world. Jesus too was willing to be of low esteem (Php.2:1-9). The remarkable thing is, that as we spend our life on others, thus giving our life away, we can find real fulfilment!

Perhaps you are still insecure and somewhat retiring - as most of us have been (see Ch.4). That certainly is nothing to be ashamed of - it can well mean that the flower of our life has not yet blossomed to the full and the best is yet to come. Growth does not come suddenly, but step by step. The Holy Spirit wants to help us open up! (Ac.4:31) We can try to reach out towards others who may be too shy to try for themselves. This is a good start; they may even be quite happy as we dare take the initiative in a short conversation or a relationship. It is best to do these things prayerfully. For it is the Holy Spirit who gives us confidence and power in our relationships, so that some of His love and glory can shine through in who we are, in what we say or do (Col.3:17).

7.5 Learning about meaningful relationships

From our deepening relationship with God, we can learn to work at meaningful relationships with other people. God has created us for a relationship with Him, and He knows better than anyone, how important meaningful relationships are! Just as Enoch "walked with God" (Gen.5:24; Hebr.11:5) in a deeply trusting relationship with Him, so God desires to have a close friendship with us. He created relationships; He knows what real faithfulness and sacrificing love are, and wants to give us His mind (1.Cor.2:16). Therefore, we can bring our needs and questions to Him, as we spend much time at His feet. Let Him be your fulfilment and your best Friend; learn friendship from Him, receiving His power to selflessly give friendship to others without desiring to receive in return. For you no longer need things "in return" - you have already received from the Lord. It is like what Mt.6:33 says: seek first God's Kingdom and his righteousness; and in the meantime, from an unselfish heart, you will receive all other things you need from God. He is our goal, and the starting point is our relationship with the Lord Jesus, and our power and strength come from Him through the Holy Spirit (Jhn.14:10-27).

A. *We can ask Him for help in restoring broken relationships* in our life. He is the Specialist. For this, it is very important that we forgive the other person, even if we feel that he or she is far more guilty in a matter than we are. Moreover, for the rebuilding and strengthening of relationships our frequent forgiveness will remain very important (Ch.8(5)). Whatever happens, we can look up to our positive and encouraging Lord, rather than on the perhaps sad or discouraging circumstances. Keep bringing problems in relationship before Him, bless in your heart the persons involved, and pray for them.

We can ask the Lord for wisdom and patience towards that specific person with a seemingly difficult character, or who never seems to agree with us. As we learn to see their heartaches or problems, it can be much easier to forgive them. Even if they have deep wounds in their lives, it may help if we give them our love and interest - and it can open the door to their hearts. Pray for an opportunity to show this; deeds are sometimes better than words.

B. *Take good care of relationships that you already have.* Look with new appreciation and understanding at the people around you, and look especially at their good qualities. Strengthen the contact you already have, and prayerfully try to develop it. If we let our own lives be enriched by walking with the Lord Jesus, we will learn precious things that can also give a quality to some of our bleak relationships. From Him, we can learn to let our contacts grow into quality relationships.

We may ask for God's wisdom when for a season there are only few meaningful relationships in our life. Perhaps we have spent too little time with the other person, or the people around us are living in spiritual poverty, looking for "important friends" (overlooking the many "normal" ones). Moreover, it may be possible that they are trying to hide their own fear behind an unreal robustness. We can ask the Lord to do something new in such contacts - and may then expectantly wait for His opportunities. Take special care and respectfully guard these new relationships! Never force yourself on others, but prayerfully wait for God's opportunities - perhaps for a meaningful conversation.

If we ourselves are open, this can help create a more open atmosphere. If a safe opportunity shows up, we can share some deeper feelings with others, thus giving them our trust. That can lower the threshold for the other person to also share something personal. However, he or she will only do so if they know that their secrets are truly safe with you. Are they?

C. *God knows that we need real friends.* We can ask the Lord to bring people on our path with which we can develop a deeper friendship - especially Christian friends with whom we can share the deep things of our lives (Ps.119:63; Prov.13:20; Gen.2:18). We can be wise and ask Him to give us the friends that He has for us. I know a young lady who did this. The Lord gave her an elderly nurse for a friend, someone much older than she was! However, she remained faithful through the years - and what a wonderful Christian this nurse turned out to be! They prayed together, reached out to colleagues together, took Malaysian students into their homes, began a Bible study, visited the sick and lonely, reached out to elderly people in their street and invited them for Christmas dinner – and now a small church has grown out of it. A price had to be paid as this young lady truly followed her guidance, but with what fruit!

Jesus Himself never ran after people to win them for Himself, and He never forced people into relationships; but He welcomed people and left the choice to them, waiting to see whom the Father would give to Him, and remaining faithful to them (Jhn.6:37-38). That example brings rest and helps us to see the people around us in a quite new perspective. However dull our situation may seem, we can receive Gods strength and joy in it to build up something good from it.

Again, it is quite important that we ask God to give us the friends of His own choice, and that we let Him fit us in the place where He wants us to be. If we follow His guidance and commission, we know that He will take care of all our needs - also with regard to finding our place in His body, the church. It often takes patience to ask for and discover His guidance, rather than forcefully preparing our own friendships. Let the Good Shepherd guide you - He knows which friends you feel at ease with, with whom you can really share; and to which ones you have something to give. It helps us to look around to see if our help is needed by anyone; we can even take the first step, if God gives us the joy to do so.

In general, we can prayerfully wait if a relationship doesn't seem to "click". Let's not cling on to it - it may not at all be your fault - perhaps the other person is going through a deep valley, has difficult family circumstances, etc. Then, we may help the person best by leaving them alone and simply pray for them (see Ch.8). God may have different things in store for them at this time. So let's not be discouraged (we simply lack the time to have intense relationships with everybody)

- yet do not give up too easily either. Again, we may ask the Lord for His counsel, as well as that of some other Christian friends who can encourage us when we need it and who can help us in our relationships. A good, deep conversation often sheds new light on the situation, and being able to pray together is a real support.

7.6 Be a real friend yourself

In order to make friends, it is important to put relationships at the top of your priority list and especially to learn to become a real friend yourself. We can all learn to place the well-being of others above our own! That is a deep and rich lesson. Friendship is something that can be sown; it can then take root at unexpected moments and places (2.Cor.9:6-7; Hos.8:7). This sowing is so important in places where little friendship can be found, or with people who have only few friends. To that end, we may develop and use whatever we have in gifts. We can ask relatives and others who know us well what our gifts are, such as helping, hospitality, listening (see Ch.6(4)).

As we build friendships, it is important to treat the other person with care and respect (arrive on time, do not change an appointment at the last minute), remaining faithful even in small things. Pray for warmth, readiness to help, wisdom, discreetness and kindness. Stand next to, not above, the other person; feel with him or her, try to be of help, and ask the Lord to guide and help you in your daily contacts.

A. *Being a listener.* Learn to listen with interest to the person concerned. Nothing is more important in friendship! There is such a need for people who really want to listen. That is good news for those who never quite know what to say... Strangely enough, to the other person the opportunity to ask questions, and to fully say what bothers him or her, may be more important than the answers we can give. It is an art to be able to listen to others and let them speak while we hold back our own ideas (it can be a sacrifice, but keep it natural and be yourself). *Listening is an art we can learn.* It is more than "hearing them": it is true interest, trying to learn and understand by short questions, and trying to feel the hopes and fears behind the words. It is more than worth it to prayerfully try this out in everyday conversations (at home or at your workplace). No one needs to know why you are asking deeper questions.

Intent listening also gives us food for prayer. We can be a blessing to those around us by just listening. It can be a healing experience for people if they can fully speak out what bothers them. We can encourage such people by asking further questions about what has just been said, for instance by repeating a short thought they just mentioned: "So your brother has hit you frequently?" They will try to see if we are "safe" to talk to, if there is space and security with us to share their heart, if they can share their insecurity or need. We can prayerfully listen and help them by being there for them. Some people have built a large circle of friends that way, but that no longer seems so important. God has given them a ministry.

Many years ago, I read in a newspaper about a lady who earned her money by listening. For a small fee, people could share their heart for an hour or so. She did not seem to speak wise words, but she listened - and she could not handle the number of people who came! This shows us something of the enormous needs in the world. Therefore, it is so important for us as Christians to learn to listen, really listen, with deep attention and respect for others and with a prayerful heart that brings their needs before God's throne, "weeping with those who weep" (Ro.12:15).

In all this, we should try to keep the conversation constructive. It does not do the other person any good to dwell on complaints, self-pity or slander. We may lovingly tell them of God's love and help. With Him, there is always hope! Now and then, we may find an opportunity to speak from our own experiences about the Lord Jesus, Who brings salvation even from loneliness and Who is always there for them. That can be friendship evangelism in the truest sense of the word.

Therefore, let's make room in our heart for others, encouraging them, showing them the bright sides of life, being a blessing without asking anything in return. Our strength and help come from the Lord Jesus.

B. *Being a helper.* We can learn to help others in many ways, such as with practical tasks. As seen above, we can also help them without words by listening. As imperfect people, we will realize that we should not allow others to become dependent on us (they will get disappointed!) but bring them closer to Jesus, Who will never disappoint them. They need to realize that their true help and strength come only from the loving heavenly Father, and that we are to depend on Him, not on people. Although our earthly friendships should be very real, they must not grow into unhealthy attachments. True friendship is unselfish and gives the other person space.

Moreover, we may help others in practical things where we can: be it cooking for a sick person, babysitting, mowing the grass for an elderly person, etc. If we also do this prayerfully for non-Christian neighbours, they may see something of the Lord Jesus in our lives. We can pray for opportunities to help others, and may soon discover that it is more blessed to give than to receive - that our life becomes more meaningful and more joyful.

C. *Being unselfish.* We can all follow the "golden rule" (Luke 6:31; Gal.5:14). A well-known Dutch saying is, "Do good and you will meet good on your path". However, the Bible goes deeper than this. Mt.7:12 says that we are to do for others what we desire that they should do for us. It is good to write down: *what exactly would we like others to do for us? Am I already doing that for others?* Initially, it may be a sacrifice for us to act that way, but God - who sees things in secret - can reward us for it (Mt.6:3-6). When we go through hard times ourselves, this way of life can be a tremendous exercise in unselfishness; we learn to give in spite of ourselves, even "at our own expense". Unselfishness can be a deep-working instrument in developing friendships. We can give of our time, our energy, our belongings - wisely and as unto the Lord, without expecting anything in return. Miss no opportunity to be good to others and bless them - to be there for them even if they are not always there for you. Doing good will become a joy to you.

7.7 *Practical openness to relationships*

We can direct our lives towards relationships in several practical ways; below are just a few suggestions.

A. *Take time for people*, make room for them in your agenda as a priority. Perhaps they come to you or phone you at unsuitable times, but they are so important – return their call as soon as possible, or make an appointment that they can look forward to (and stick to it!). We often need to make some fundamental changes: knowing that *people are more important than things*... Jesus gave people his full attention and directed Himself towards them. Often, we are so locked into our own world that we may dislike a break into our privacy. Our visitors may then feel unwanted, unwelcome, discouraged. Jesus always has an eye for people, wanting to help them in their needs. Therefore, it is good for us to learn to be available to people and give them of our time. Personally, I did not always find this easy - but it is what Jesus would have done. (Jhn.6:35-38)

Opening up to others and sharing our heart with them will become easier once we learn to see how very precious we ourselves are in God's sight (Ch.5 & 6). That makes it easier for us to notice the deep value of those around us, and that appreciation will shine through in our actions. It will build them up!

B. *Take an interest in people*. Often, this will take some effort, love and self-sacrifice. If a conversation deals with items in the life of the other person, there may be little or no attention left for you. However, God can take care of you very well! If He brings people to you, He gives you strength to be involved with them and to be open to whatever concerns them.

It also helps to remember - if we can - the names, birthdays, family circumstances etc. of people we meet. I once knew a busy person who wrote down the names of all the children of acquaintances and relatives in his address book. In this time of anonymity and mass-mentality it is important that people know that they matter and are "special".

C. *Go to church activities and events*; do not miss them if you can, for at such events it can be easier to develop contacts and friendships. It is likely that you will meet the people there very often, enabling you to develop some friendships. Helping out at such events - pouring coffee etc. - are good and natural occasions to start a conversation with them. Usually, they like to have volunteers!

Once we get to know some caring and reliable people there, it may be good to tell them of our loneliness. Just discussing it can alleviate our hurting feelings, and it especially helps if we can pray with them. Their wisdom, understanding, and experience can be valuable to us and build us up in areas where we want to grow.

D. *Ask for God's agenda* for your life. In your church there may be less opportunities to meet others, but you can ask the Lord (His guidance is important) if it would be good to also join Christian activities outside the church, like some interdenominational Bible study, or to join a choir or missions prayer group. It can also help to take a useful course or visit Christian conferences. Summer activities in evangelism, in which we get involved practically together for the same goal, can teach us how to join forces together and get along with others! In joint activities, charity, or volunteer work, there are many opportunities. In this, we can develop friendships and an interest in people.

7.8 Getting active in making contacts

If we become interested in others, we do not just make contacts for our own sake, but also for the sake of the other person. It is worthwhile to remember that we may fail and even hurt others by withdrawing from relationships with them! Many people feel that they are not of value to others. Nothing is less true. One reason for not seeing this can be that the other person is ashamed of showing a need for friendship and affection. We are to be sensitive towards them, not forcing ourselves upon them but prayerfully waiting for an opening. We know from experience how very necessary friendships are, and we can become instruments to help those whom God places on our path. Let Him choose our friends - having friends has many and deep consequences! Make it a matter of prayer and ask for His help. Some opportunities can be:

A. *Visiting others who are lonely*, or those who are not "in" with the crowd (Mt.5:46; 22:8-10; Rom.12:1-5). Can we love even the "unlovable"? Jesus did. As we have experienced loneliness ourselves, we can more easily feel their hurts and learn to comfort them (2.Cor.1:4). During meetings, it helps to start looking for people who are in the background or less popular, but also for those who by their loud appearance or by trying to impress may inwardly scream, "love me!" Accept them as they are, if necessary point others to their good qualities (find those out!), and make an effort to get them accepted by the group. Pray for them, stand next to them as a real and faithful friend. That will encourage them, and precious relationships may result.

In the past, we may have sought to be with the popular crowd - with those who had friends enough and did not need our friendship as much as those in the background. It is good to remember that those who have many friends can often spend only little time and attention on us. If you yourself are a real friend, your goal is not achieving some status or being "in", but you are prepared for sacrificial giving and deep relationships. Let Jesus be your example, Who found his friends not among those of high stature or among religious leaders, but among sick, weak, even sinful people. His love was truly unselfish. What we give to the "least" among us, *that* is what we have truly done unto Him (Mt.25:34-40)! Do we want to live for Him? If we visit such people and become real friends to them, God will teach us compassion, and we can grow in relationships that do not just take away our loneliness, but that are also meaningful for His Kingdom.

By starting to love other lonely people, some very strong and lasting friendships may develop - even so many that we can hardly find the time to visit all their birthday parties!

B. *Open your doors in hospitality.* Just think of what would be possible in your situation. If you feel insecure, buy a book on hospitality and good manners; however, many people know as little about it as you do! Be always open to receiving guests - make a supply for it (cookies, canned foods, nice table cloths etc.). Try to keep your living room tidy and cosy, so that you will feel secure when unexpected guests ring the doorbell. If you love cooking, regularly ask people to lunch or dinner. If you are not a real talker, then ask two or three people at the same time! You can be a real blessing that way. If you have little opportunity to cook, you can ask people for coffee, for instance after the church service. You can ask the same person to come again, and if they seem to appreciate this and ask you back, you could also ask them to join you for a concert or outing. For other lonely people this can be so important, especially if this is not just a single event and your love and commitment become apparent over the months and years.

In all this, ask the Lord for His openings, act prayerfully, and make your guests feel welcome. Especially those who spend much time at home can appreciate such an invitation. It is good to let them know how much you appreciate their visit; this will help them feel that they are welcome and take away their shyness. In our village, we had an elderly single man (my mother knew him through "meals on wheels") who had lots of visitors, because he kept telling people how excited he was about their visit!

C. *Visit others*, especially the elderly and sick, not only in your family but also neighbours and people from the church (Mt.25:36). This is often a sensitive and impressionable time in their life, in which they may especially appreciate visitors and can be open to a good and deep conversation, even about Christian things. It also works the other way around: people who have been sick for a long time, or pensioners who spend much time alone and may at times feel useless

- they have time for meaningful conversations, and we can *ask their advice* about things that bother us. They often have much knowledge of life and more time for intercession - things so precious and rare in our days! Why not benefit from all that God can give us through them? It can give new colour to their life to be encouraging and meaningful to others; and we can learn from them. However, even if they are too sick to give us anything, they are important for the special person they are. Be a blessing to them, take some flowers or a fruit basket in return from time to time. Do everything to make it a nice visit; should the other person not feel well or keep complaining, try to encourage them. It can be helpful to pray together if they are open to that; for their true strength is in the Lord (Ex.15:2; Ps.18:32; 138:3; Hab.3:19; 2.Cor.12:9; Jam.5:16).

D. *Be faithful in your correspondence.* Never lay a letter aside without answering it - if a specific question is asked, reply preferably within one week. Sending birthday- and Christmas cards is a great way to show those who do not live very near that you remember and appreciate them. If you have little time, it is ideal to add a (copied) personal newsletter to Christmas cards, so that people know how you are doing. However, do not be disappointed if for a season people do not write or visit you. They may be very busy or go through some trial, and your understanding may help them. After some time, just send them a nice card. Do not complain but rather ask them how they are doing and let them know that you are interested in them. Sick and elderly people may especially enjoy your mail. It is worth it looking for really beautiful or funny cards (or make these yourself) so that they are at hand when needed. With cards, you can bless others in many creative ways, and a card can be written so easily...

7.9 Helping others to develop more relationships

If we help those around us to develop more relationships, we can bear fruit out of our own experiences with the Lord and with other people, even if we lose a few friends that way. Put your treasured friendships in your open hand, for

God to work on as He pleases. It can be helpful to invite a few lonely people together to your home (for a meal, for a birthday party, for a good walk or trip), if you feel they could become a blessing to each other. If this turns out well, you could repeat it, also encouraging them to visit one another (Peter left his pen here, would you mind bringing it to him as you go home? Laura is sick, I'm sure she would enjoy it if you visit her! This postcard is also for Joan and Lisa; would you mind passing it on to them?).

We can help others as we try to take away the loneliness around us that we ourselves found so hard to bear. Through our own battles, we can understand others so well and give them advice from our own experience. That way, even those battles can bear rich fruit!

8
HANDLING PROBLEMS IN RELATIONSHIPS

In our busy world, where people often lack the time to meet each other, problems in relationships seem on the increase. It is precisely here that we find some of the greatest challenges if we wish to obey the Lord! Although every situation is different, there are some Biblical principles to help us. God can use such situations to build our character and to teach us precious lessons in courage, love, faith and endurance.

Some of the following thoughts may be helpful in your specific situation.

8.1 A practical approach to problems

A. *Focus on getting the relationship restored*. We can choose to keep working towards full restoration, with a firm decision of our will, as we pray for God's help. Relationships are precious in God's sight and worth fighting for! Past events may have so wounded us that we just want to get rid of our pain, and prefer not to meet the other person - to avoid even the memory of that pain. Even though this is understandable, God's goal for us (in as far as it depends on us) is that relationships will be soundly restored. We can pray for His wisdom regarding the circumstances, and where necessary ask others (such as a pastor or elder we can trust) for help. Relationships are very precious to God. We ourselves were once far away from Him, yet He did not try to soothe His own pain but went out to find and redeem us. God even gave up His own Son to restore our relationship with Him and to bring us to repentance. His loving heart waits for us with open arms! We can see in this what high priority relationships have with Him. Let Him be our example. Jesus had no guilt, and yet He took the first step towards us who hurt Him. He went a lowly way, in love and openness, and that way led Him to victory (Php.2:5-9; Eph.5:1-2).

B. *When others criticize us, let us keep our hearts open.* It is not easy to pray for restoration of a relationship if others have really wounded us, for instance, by their criticism (or if we have wounded them!). But if we shy away from them, or don't mention our own opinion and go along with them to win their acceptance; or if we defend ourselves or want to get our rights, or even pay them back evil for evil, then we do not deal with the problem correctly - and the problem remains. It is better to discover the way that Jesus taught us. Let's open up ourselves to God and ask Him for His opinion of other people's points of criticism. We will then not immediately accept that the criticism is true and - if it turns out to be true indeed - that God and man would no longer want us. For when it is true, it becomes an aid to our inner growth! (Prov.15:32) However, if their criticism is not true, we can bring it to the Lord and leave it with Him.

It is important to openly meet both the other person and the problem (Ch.8(9), Ch.2(8)). It will not help us to reason the problem away or deny it altogether, or if we shy away from the other person - or "act" like nothing is wrong. *If we are prepared to truly deal with our own sins, we will not be afraid to openly go and speak to others and to hear even their criticism, for God will help us!* That way, the accuser of our lives will not get a foothold, and the criticism of others will help you to discover the weak spots in your spiritual armor and make you strong. As you are prepared to be vulnerable, you are less of a threat to the other person, you "disarm" him or her, and it becomes easier for them to establish a relationship with you. Many people respond from their own wounded lives, and when their hurts are revealed, we usually don't need to take that personally. We can recognize that by the fact that such a person will behave towards others the same way as towards us.

However, we can do our best to love him or her, to pray, and to be patient with them. That way, we can grow in unity, in spite of human differences. Nobody will share all of our opinions, and yet we can still have many friends. Those with differing opinions are the ones we can learn from; their opinions can test us and even add something significant to our lives.

C. *If we criticize others, we are responsible ourselves*; and we are the only ones who can change that. The best thing to do is, to come to the Lord and ask His forgiveness for our own criticism. If we have wronged other people, we may also need to ask for their forgiveness. In cases where others have wronged us, the matter concerns us, and in many cases need to talk this over with them. We can only do that in the right spirit, from a heart of love, and for this we need the Lord more than in any other matter I know of! Therefore, prayerfully bring the person concerned to Him, asking for His love in your heart as you try to work towards restoration, and for His help in finding a good opportunity to speak with them. This is a difficult step, but it is very important that we take it.

8.2 Ask the Comforter to help you see things rightly

The Holy Spirit can convince us deep in our heart of our own part in the problem (Jhn.16:8). We need not immediately accept that every problem that comes our way is somehow our fault. We often tend to accept accusations (by the enemy of our souls, or by other people) for things that were not really our fault. However, we also tend to shy away from facing any guilt that we *do* have - because we are fearful, or with the excuse: "that was just a small thing; it is not so important, it happened by accident". We should then realize that to other people those "details" may be very important, and we may need to open up to God to point these things out to us. Real honesty is so important! Even though criticism by others may be thrown at us in words of bitterness (God never acts that way), these words may still contain some precious advice and can be a blessing in disguise. Let's make sure we benefit from any truth in it...

A. When we have sinned

It is always good to ask ourselves against whom we have sinned: against the Lord, or also against others? A good rule is, that we only ask others for forgiveness if we have sinned against them - so we can say, "John, it was me who damaged your car" - and make up for it in any way we should. But we should not say, "John, you think that I like you, but I want to ask forgiveness for the fact that I often hate you in my heart" - that way, we can do more harm than good! For then we have first of all sinned against the Lord and need to put things right with Him and pray for a change of our heart and attitude; the other person may never even know, and we do not want to hurt them but build towards a good relationship in the future. Therefore, it is better to confess any wrong words, deeds, and attitudes towards others, without burdening them with any sinful feelings. Feelings can be quite unreliable; they are part of our personal battle of faith, and we wrestle them through with the Lord. For our real sins (things that we have clearly seen to be wrong or thoughtless or insensitive), therefore, we first of all need to ask God to forgive us, and only if necessary we ask the other person to forgive us as well.

Asking forgiveness is not easy, but it is mostly the only way to put things right with others, as we disregard our pride and take the first step towards them (Mt.5:23) - even though we may feel that the other person has more guilt! We can ask forgiveness for our part, however small, and it will clear up the situation if we go to others to talk and get things out of the way, admitting our own imperfections. Others may then feel free to admit their part in the problem.

Restored relationships are so important. God sacrificed his only Son to restore the relationship with us, and He bore no guilt! He gave His utmost to restore that relationship; do we act in the same way towards others? A truly open conversation (in all confidentiality) can work out deep things in a relationship. Such openness may need to come from us first, and we may have to show our weakness in it; but even if the other person responds negatively and our efforts seem fruitless, we do it out of our love towards the Lord and He knows this. If our relationship with Him has been restored, we may hand the result of our efforts towards others over to Him.

B. When others have sinned

If we remain close to the Lord, we will grow in discernment. *The truth will set us free* (Jhn.8:32). In certain cases, where we think that the other person has clearly sinned against us, it is mostly right to tell him or her so in humility and love (see Ch.8(9)). If we are not quite sure what to do, we can ask another trusted Christian about it, for instance a pastor or elder; but we must not slander the person concerned. Sometimes, the sins of others are not for us to deal with (unless God clearly brings the matter on our path so that we can warn them), such as when it concerns things that we are not involved in personally (a sin not against us, for instance: the neighbors have a bad marriage and keep quarreling). However, we do pray for them! In other cases, the time may not be right (the sinner is celebrating his birthday, or in a hospital ward, etc.). The case can be a very serious one that would be better for the police or a pastor to deal with, and you may discuss this with them. However, if the sin clearly concerns you (you are almost certain that John damaged your car, and it wrecks your relationship with him), you can - after prayer - ask him in private about the impression you have, without claiming off-hand that he is guilty - unless, of course, you saw the event with our own eyes (Mt.18:15-17). Only the Lord can judge the deepest motives of others. Perhaps John did this unknowingly or acted in revenge for a sin we committed against him; or perhaps he has been sorry for a long time and lacked the courage to tell us... We may keep an eye on the eternal salvation of the other person, especially if he or she does not yet know Jesus. We will not allow our strained relationship to stand in the way of others getting to know Jesus. We need much of His grace in such situations. Is our attitude in this matter such, that the other person can see Jesus' love and acceptance in us? Our attitude speaks louder than our most beautiful words!

C. Finding the true benefit

In the end, if people accuse us, we may well be able to do something constructive with their remarks, so that this can be a time of personal growth. True friends take the courage to show us our sinful behavior; but if the other person has no intentions towards real friendship, and we cannot find any guilt even after bringing it before the Lord, then this still remains a good lesson in learning to forgive and accept others in their imperfections. It is a battle, a choice we have to keep making all the time. It is important that we don't let ourselves be accused by the enemy any longer, but that we assure ourselves of our security in the Lord! (Col.1:11-14; Rom.8:1,31-35; 2.Cor.5:17) This does not come automatically, but we can learn to hold on to the truth that He has forgiven our sins and that we can stand before Him as cleansed people. That in itself is a great source of security and joy (Ps.16:8,11) in the midst of problems.

8.3 Openness through forgiveness

Forgiveness is a choice. We can help restore a relationship by forgiving the other person fully in our heart, for all that has hurt us or for what we see as wrong. It is best to do so as soon as possible (Eph.4:26), even before going to him or her to discuss this matter in love and truth. If we have this commitment to forgive, then we can let them know that we fully work towards for the restoration and continuation of the relationship. That is not easy, and with deep wounds it may - in the beginning - be necessary to daily speak out our willingness to forgive towards the Lord (or whenever the old bitter thoughts come up). This attitude can grow into a continuing choice to forgive. Such choices become easier, the more we make them!

Forgiveness can be a process. Our wounds may not be healed instantly - not because we are unfaithful Christians, but because we still hurt and our hearts need time to heal. We do not need to force restoration on a relationship, but may maintain openness, and by our commitment to forgive create a good climate for healing the pain of both parties. Forgiving can become a good habit, almost as natural as breathing. We can choose it as the way to take in every event or thought regarding others.

The following considerations may help us to forgive:

A. *Consider any alleviating circumstances.* We can consider the difficulties in the life of the other person that may make him or her tense and irritable. These can be things from the past we know nothing about, even though we have known the person for some time - just like they may know nothing of the painful events and hardships in our life! Such moderating circumstances help us to encounter the other person with mercy and compassion, even though they may not be open to this yet because of their hurting feelings. That is why we need to love others first of all, even though we need to tell them that they sinned against us (Ch.8(9)). It is good to pray for an opportunity to do this, in a way that does not threaten them, so that correction can fall on fruitful soil. However, depending on the person, we may need to be firm, precisely because we love them and want the best for them. Their response may not immediately be right and we may need to hold on - yet striving towards full restoration.

The foundation for a good and trusting relationship can best be laid in times of few real difficulties. Sometimes, today's problems result from yesterday's negligence. However, it is never too late to start building a relationship, in which love and forgiveness are the most important building blocks. Love is not using sweet words, it is a commitment and responsibility for the other person - at times love can even be very firm! Love does not look for what it can get out of a relationship but cares enough to give (Ac.20:35). Love is a *choice*, just like forgiveness - not because the other person deserves this, but out of grace, just as Jesus has loved and forgiven us (Col.3:13; Eph.4:32; 1.Jhn.4:7-8, 20-21; Rom.15:7).

B. *Keep choosing to forgive.* Jesus hated sin yet loved the sinners – He even died in their place to redeem them from sin. If the sins of others are truly there, it is then that they truly need our forgiveness! Let us not harbor any bitterness - it works negatively even if we never speak it out; it harms both our relationships and us. Choose against bitterness and bring your hurts to the Lord. If we do not become bitter people, but learn to accept the other imperfect and perhaps wounded person (however many tears that may cost us), we can learn to forgive at a deeper level. It is easier to forgive others for things that happened by accident, or if they come to us to ask for forgiveness; but many do not have the courage and may push their guilt away. The more the other person is at wrong, the more our forgiveness is necessary. Do not keep this from them, even if the pain is still in your heart, and if their improvement seems slow. The Bible asks us to forgive, and to love our enemies (Mt.5:44; 6:14-15).

Should the sinful situation remain in the life of the other person even after we have spoken to him or her in love (Ch.8(9)), then we need to keep praying for much faith in our own heart, and for the work of the Holy Spirit in the heart of that person. That always is a good thing to pray for, even if we do not understand certain people or their situation at all. God knows the hearts and needs. If God has given us love and acceptance, we can pray for an opportunity to talk things over and to admonish them where needed (Ch.8(9)).

As we have seen, forgiveness and love are a choice of our will. *Every choice is like speaking to our heart*; our feelings may follow only later, but they will come around more easily as we continue to choose doing what Jesus would do.

C. *Dare to let go.* If restoration of the relationship is not yet in sight, keep praying and forgiving; but let God do the work and *do not keep fretting over it* or trying to force a restoration into existence while the other person is not yet ready for it. A wound needs cleanliness and rest. If we keep fumbling with it, this can delay the healing. The enemy may try to keep us fruitless as we spend too much energy on our worries, and we can send him away in the name of Jesus. We can then let go and give both the other person and our worrisome thoughts to God. This certainly is not easy, but we can trust

God's work in the life of that person; He is well able to bring it to completion (Ps.138:8; Is.42:16, 65:1; Jud.:24).

Also, let's not make this worrisome relationship into some kind of an idol by looking at it continually, but let's ask God what His goals for us are as we focus on Him. We may not "own" anyone. It can be painful to let go of a friend for a longer period, but this can be wholesome - also for that friend. Give the relationship away to God. It helps us to let go of the problem by realizing that, once we have done everything towards restoration, the problem is now solely His. Our priority is not any earthly relationship, but the relationship with God. It will help us to spend some extra time with the Lord, deepening our relationship with Him and being rich in Him (Lk.12:13-21). People may disappoint us, but the Lord is so faithful!

In a very painful situation in my life, I once had great difficulty in forgiving a certain person. My thoughts kept circling around the problem, even though I did not want to. Then, the Lord showed me that I could only become free from it by forgiving totally. We do not forgive people by finding "excuses" for them, but because something really *did* go wrong! When, with the help of God, I did speak out forgiveness, it was as if the Lord Jesus was standing between that person and me, so that my inner eyes could no longer see the person but only the Lord! Those sins had been "covered"...

Later on, when I remembered person, I knew: God is at work, but that is not my task - I may cast myself upon Him in this situation. He wants to forgive, save, and restore that other person. He desires unity in His body. We may receive His compassion for such wounded people, learn to bless them and to trust God to continue His work in the heart and life of this person.

In extremely difficult cases, where we find it hard to forgive and to keep forgiving, it can help to ask prayer from two experienced counselors (perhaps an elder in the church and his wife) to pray about the situation together, and to speak out forgiveness before two such "witnesses" (Dt.19:15; Mt.18:16) who can establish the fact that we did confess bitterness and decided to forgive. Should the enemy later on attack us over this with feelings of guilt, their witness will settle the matter, even if the other person is not willing to talk things over or to forgive. Moreover, these witnesses can keep praying that forgiveness remain established in your heart in the time to come.

D. *Take your time.* We can use this time to learn to find our strength in the Lord and healing for our emotions, and to discover the new things God has for us at this time. Even now, life has it's good sides. God has given us talents and possibilities. We can learn to enjoy the things we *do* have! Seek out those good things and focus on these so that they grow in your heart. That way, the problems gradually lose their sting and fade into the background.

Sometimes, because of our own pain, we cannot handle the relationship with the other person very well. If so, it may be right to remain somewhat in the background for a season. We do not need to force ourselves to do things we cannot handle, but also we do not need to flee from pain. It is better to find real causes and true healing by seeking help from a counselor who knows how to keep a secret.

Some emotions take time to heal. God does take time with us, but also with the other person. He does a thorough work, not a superficial one. Let Him be our Guide, and let's not get in the way by saying or doing things that He does not ask from us, such as forcing ourselves upon the other person while he or she is still unable to handle or appreciate the relationship. We are too precious for that, and it is better to spend our time and efforts His way. Jesus never forced Himself on anyone in His zeal to restore the relationship with us - even though that was precisely the reason why He came to earth! As long as our relationship with the other person is not fully restored, he or she may find it difficult to accept anything from us until their pain is completely healed. In the mean time, we can always find guidance in the

Word of God. (Rom.12:18-19, 13:8; Eph.4:31-32; 1.Pet.2:19-23, 4:12-19)

8.4 Becoming sensitive towards the feelings of others

Sometimes, others will respond negatively to us, and when that happens it can be good to ask ourselves what the reason may be. They may respond from in inner wound, caused by events in the past (perhaps not even by us but by others, for instance in their youth). Perhaps our attitude has - unintentionally - awakened that old pain. It is good to ask the Lord, "Have I done anything in the past that caused a hurt?" - even if we never intended any wrong. Did we consider the hurts and weaknesses and the personal situation of the other person, in as far as we knew them? It is so important to *ask the Lord* about this (rather then brooding over the situation or digging into our heart and past), so that the enemy - who is an accuser - cannot use this opportunity to bring any false guilt upon us. That robs us of our joy and does not help our relationships...

We can grow in sensitivity by frequently asking God, "Lord, will you make me sensitive towards those that I meet?" I once knew a young man who did this every day, and the practicality of it struck me. It is not hard to do; and we can grow in this by regularly praying for others, by thinking of them with respect as created by God under His responsibility, and by trying to imagine how we would feel in their circumstances. If we have suffered much ourselves, this can help us to imagine how others feel; I noticed this in the life of some pastoral workers. By getting the victory in the battles of our own life we can later help others in such areas with insight and compassion.

Some people may hurt us in our sensitivity and openness, and then it seems we cannot help or even reach them because we feel hurt. At such times, it may be good to hand the person over to the care of the Lord. Perhaps the Lord will use someone else in that situation. And we can bring our tears to Him - He is such a wonderful, sensitive Comforter!

8.5 Truth in the mirror

Praying for love towards the other person is one of the best things we can do (1.Cor.13:12-13). It will not help us or anyone else if we judge and criticize others (Rom.2:1-4; 14:1-13; Jam.2:13; 4:11-12). Many of us know from experience how painful and destructive criticism towards us has been. Thus, we can understand how badly we can discourage and wound others with our negative remarks. How can we change? An English lady in my Bible College days gave good advice:

"God has not given us a spirit of criticism, but of intercession".

What a deep truth that is! If we pray for them, we can learn to see the other person with eyes of hope. Paul (1.Cor.13:5-7) teaches us to always think the best of others. Only God truly knows their heart and their weaknesses, however much we feel that he or she is wrong. Never think that you fully understand their background or present situation. We hardly ever do.

A. The mirror of our soul

It helps to take time to look at ourselves as in a mirror regarding the negative points we appear to see in others. What are *we* like in this respect? We can often "find" those things in others to the measure we "recognize" them from our own life - that means, we ourselves are not truly free from this... and we think that they will respond just as we do, whereas that may not even be true! We even throw accusations at them, like the stones in Jhn.8:7. Therefore, it is worthwhile to ask the Lord, as soon as you get irritated about the sin of someone else: "Lord, why do I recognize this? Can it be that you want to speak to me, rather than to the other person?" Mt.7:1-5 has very enlightening things to say on this. In the Netherlands, we have a proverb saying, "as the inn-keeper is, so he trusts his guests"! How would we do as inn-keepers? What are our expectations of others; do we judge them from our own sinful heart or from some bad experiences in the past? How do we trust others - *what* do we seem to recognize in them from our own sinful thoughts? Can we clearly recognize who they are, as long as we have some of that same sin? We cannot be of much help then... until we come to the Lord for cleansing.

B. The mirror in other people

For the reasons above, it can be helpful for us to develop precisely those things that we seem to miss in others, rather than criticizing them. That way, we can both fill up the gap of our own shortcomings and may have something good to give to those around us - in sensitivity, generosity, affection, servitude. If others accuse us of certain sins that in all honesty we do not see in ourselves, this will still help us improve on that point because the other person may just seem to "recognize" his own weaknesses in us. He or she may need us to act from the "opposite spirit" (Ch.8(7)) to receive help and healing (Mt.5:39; Rom.12:20-21). Their loveless accusations may stem from their own problems and hardships. But even if their words are true only partly - say, 20% - these give us a tremendous reason for change!

If we easily criticize others, we may also easily criticize ourselves. Perhaps we have not seen ourselves as a precious creation of he Lord - and that may make it hard to also see others that way! We may look at ourselves with God's eyes of mercy, and can learn to forgive and love ourselves by choosing to do so again and again (1.Pet.2:9-10; 1.Jhn.3:19-21). Then, it will become easier to also forgive and love others around us. It helps to ask God to show us more of His goodness. By frequently thanking Him for all the precious gifts and possibilities He has given us (Ch.6), we can learn to see more of God's beautiful design in the life of other people. Did you ever think of that, when you had a relationship problem?

Perhaps it can be a help to make a list of all the good qualities that are visible in the other "difficult" person, in spite of everything (Php.2:3). Try to approach that person in a constructive manner. We can rejoice in what God has already given to him or her, and thank Him for His creation. Imagine being in heaven one day, together with that person - then cleansed, restored, loving - what a beautiful child of God! All sins will be gone and all tears will be wiped away; we will then see one another with loving eyes as God's children. Thinking of others in this way can restore our hope and faith for them and widen our hearts, even if they have not yet seen their need to face the truth. In spite of the difficult present, we can thus radiate more easily something of the tremendous perspective for this person in God's Kingdom.

Of course, any criticism expressed by others – what they see in us - can also work as a mirror which they hold before us (as in Ch.8(2c)) and that we can indeed benefit from, but here we want to show another side of their mirror - what we see in them - that we can constructively be involved with.

C. The mirror of the Word

The more we read the Word of God, His personal counsel to us, the more we will understand of what He desires for us and our relationships. The Bible has quite a few helpful chapters on relationships to read and practice (perhaps one chapter each day from the books below, taking you just over a month), such as Mt.5-7; Jhn.17; Ro.12-16; Gal.6; Eph.4-6; Php.4; Col.3-4; 1.Thess.5; 2.Thess.3; 1.Tim.6; Tit.3; Hebr.12-13; Jam.3-5; 1.Pet.2-5; 1.Jhn.1-4.

D. Becoming a mirror of God

In the end, what we keep looking at is what we will look like – we begin to reflect it. We cannot change ourselves, but the more we look up to our loving heavenly Father and His glory, the more we are changed into His likeness (1.Cor.13:12; 1.Cor.15:49; 2.Cor.3:18;). What a great reflection for our mirror! If we remain very close to Jesus, we can also come closer to one another. It is He who works out healing in us and our relationships, and teaches us how we can handle difficult situations (Mt.22:37-40; Ps.25:12-15; Ro.8:28). Do we spend enough time with Him, asking for His opinion?

Problems with relationships can bring us to our knees before God, and He can mould our personality in an area of hidden weakness.

8.6 *An attitude to bless*

It is not always easy to bless others, especially if they behave in an unfriendly or hostile manner towards us. The Bible shows what we can do if people are hostile (Lk.6:27-29; Mt.5:43-48; Rom.12:14-21). It is frequently true that those who seem to be against us are people with deep problems. That is precisely the time in their life when they need our love the most, even though they may never admit it.

I once noticed that it can be very effective to whisper (very softly, so that the other person can *not* hear it): "I choose to love you", whenever you meet someone who is unfriendly towards you. Someone had given me that advice, and although it seemed incredible to me that this would work, I tried this out during a time of need, and it did! Perhaps the reason is that we keep choosing right then and there for an attitude to bless, and that when we meet him or her the other person senses that there is room for them in our life. It can be like breaking through some old pattern, as if they feel that our heart is right towards them even though they cannot hear what we whisper. By doing this, we make sure that our heart is right; we are building on a good foundation, even though part of our own hurts may still be there.

If we frequently sit at Jesus' feet, He teaches us both a right attitude and what it means to have a relationship under His blessing. As we come close to Him, we can also come closer to the other person that He has created for His glory.

As we pray for our enemies, we can also ask God to bless them - not in the things they may presently do wrong, but for instance by praying prayers like:

> "Lord, will You bless Your work in the heart of this person, will you enlarge the room You have in their heart";

"Bless him (or her) with the beautiful sense of Your presence";

"Make him a tree of righteousness";

"Give her a deep worship towards You";

"Lord, please fill this person with hope and joy, and with Your Holy Spirit";

"Will You, in the midst of pain, give this person the courage for a conversation";

"Let this person feel safe with You and from there receive space to grow in relationships"; "Lord, fulfill Your beautiful purpose in the life of this precious person; make that all the abilities You gave them will shine for Your glory";

"Make this person a blessing to others, a pillar in Your Kingdom";

"Increase Your glory through this life"; or simply:

"Lord, will You give this person a nice day".

When the problems are very deep indeed, we may not know what to pray, but if the Lord has given us the ability to speak in tongues, we can pray that way as we bring the person before His throne in intercession - the Holy Spirit can then pray through us, even with sighs too deep for words (Rom.8:26-28).

As we can see, praying frequently for the other person is very important, especially when he or she seems hostile. Perhaps the other person keeps struggling with a personal problem because we did not pray. As long as there is a burden on our heart because of a relationship problem with them, it is good to keep praying, not so much, "Lord, convince this person of how wrong he was" (we let God do the judging, and let the Holy Spirit do the convincing) (Rom.14:4,12-13; Jhn.16:7-8), but from an attitude that prays for everything that is good towards the other person, as we would wish things to be for ourselves - heaping blessings on them, as it were (Mt.7:12, 22:39). The more we do this, the more God can prepare our heart for the often unexpected things He wants to do in our lives in the future. Can we trust Him to finish His work in the other person as He does it in us (Rom.9:28; Jud.:21-24)?

Finally, we can ask God to show us ways to become a practical blessing to the other person. That could be: repairing a flat tire, helping to do the dishes, bring them a cup of coffee, do an errand. It is does not matter so much what it is, as long as we start seeing the possibilities that God brings to our attention to be a blessing to others.

8.7 Acting in the "opposite spirit"

St. Francis of Assisi wrote a well-known prayer that can be a great help to us:

> "Lord, make me an instrument of Your peace,
> let me bring love where hatred abounds,
> let me bring forgiveness where there have been insults,
> let me bring unity where there are conflicts,
> let me bring truth where people err,
> let me bring faith where there is doubt,
> let me bring hope where hope seems lost,
> let me bring light where darkness reigns,
> let me bring joy where there is sadness.
>
> In all this, may I seek
> not so much to be comforted, but to comfort,
> not so much to be understood, but to understand,
> not so much to be loved, but to love.
>
> For it is by giving that we receive,
> and by losing ourselves that we find,
> and by forgiving that we receive forgiveness,
> and by dying that we are raised to eternal life."

This is a very meaningful way to change our attitude. Many of us tend to flee situations where we feel coldness of heart, but we can bring warmth and care; when people put each other down, we can bring encouragement and build them up; where there is greed, we can bring unselfishness and generosity. That means: a giving, open and disarming attitude that even turns "the other cheek" (Lk.6:27-31). I once learned a lesson when I made an irritable remark to a Nigerian student in our Bible College. He responded in great courtesy and was exceptionally friendly to me, providing for my needs, passing me the sugar before I asked, etc. - while fiery coals assembled on my head (Mt.5:44-48; Ro.12:20)! How ashamed I was under his meek response. His example spoke louder than all of my study books. The Holy Spirit was at work and convicted me.

A. How can we learn to respond in the "opposite spirit"? (Rom.12:20-21).

(a) Firstly, the Holy Spirit wants to teach us and give us confidence; He is the Spirit Who is truly opposite to the "spirit of this world". Therefore, it is good to pray frequently for the infilling of the Holy Spirit, for His strength and insight (Jhn.14:26; Eph.1:17-18). Because He inspires and supports us, we can learn to respond to unkind people in a friendly and courteous manner, keeping the communication lines open to prepare a restoration of the relationship.

(b) Rather than simply looking at the negative aspects in a given situation, it will help us to write down what *good* things seem to be missing. Instead of avoiding that situation or getting irritated, we can then *prayerfully try to fill the gaps* of those lacking good things with an "opposite attitude", asking for God's help and guidance. Doing the right thing in such situations may not be easy but it can mean a breakthrough in God's battlefields.

At the same time, this is an excellent way to deal with our own weaknesses on that point as well as to have a good influence on the situation. It is necessary that we have already brought our own sins at that given point (let's say, in a situation where people strive for a high position and honor) to the Lord Jesus, so that we can respond out of God's forgiveness in our own life (and, therefore, from His authority and strength rather than our own).

Sometimes God wants us to give the best part to others, as with Abraham in the important matter of dividing the land, who gave the first choice to Lot (Gen.13). However, we will experience, like Abraham, that God blesses us as we obey Him!

Many years ago, on a vacation, I met a young lady that kept putting me down before the group. That did hurt! I decided to try hard to respond lovingly, for instance by asking her if I could bring her something from the village shop, or if she was interested in joining us for a walk (even though I was almost certain she would not come with us), or by drawing her into the group. Amazingly, it did work! Her attitude changed totally. Later on, it appeared that her well-to-do parents had given her beautiful clothes but never paid much attention to her as a person; this must have been the reason why my attitude and attention had a healing effect on her. People who have received little love in their life, can easily feel insecure or threatened, which can turn into rebellion. We may help them tremendously by giving them love and, if we pray God for a natural opening to do so, by pointing them to our never failing Friend: Jesus.

One day, we will harvest what we sow. Instead of harvesting bitterness and depressing thoughts, let us therefore sow love, joy, peace, and the other fruits of the Holy Spirit (Gal.5:22-23; 6:7-9; 2.Cor.9:6-8; Mt.26:52) in the situation in which we find ourselves. We can do this by becoming a cleansed channel for the Holy Spirit and by asking Him to work through us, as we open ourselves up to Him.

(c) Furthermore, it can help us to imagine *how the Lord Jesus in His love would see the other person*, what He would have done in the situation, and then to do what He would have done. This is something we need to choose for repeatedly, for this does not happen automatically! Like Jesus, we must learn to lay down our life. We can ask Him what would glorify Him in this situation. We do not need to receive from people and what they think, but only from God - He alone is the source of all our blessings.

Some people we meet may not act from unwillingness but from their inability to act correctly. The only love they experience at this moment may be ours! A *good example* can be a real inspiration and is much easier to follow in practice than a good *theory*. We can become such good examples by our deep love relationship with the Lord Jesus. A clean heart is also the best preparation for being open towards others and giving them our attention.

The darkness can only disappear as we switch on the light. We do not need to fight the darkness; God will fight for us as we let His light shine through us. His presence brings the victory! We can learn to open ourselves up to the Holy Spirit, rather than fighting against "flesh and blood" (Eph.6:12; 2.Cor.5:16-17)), so that He will dispel the darkness. We may realize that those around us, too, are involved in the fight against the enemy of our souls and that they need our prayers. God loves the sinner, even though He hates sin. We too may separate these, as we look around us. We can then pray for and encourage those involved in the struggle. It is also good to remember, that as we love the least of our brothers and sisters, we love Jesus Himself - that is a very deep Scriptural truth... (Mt.25:40-45; 1.Jhn.4:20-21)

8.8 Guarding our thoughts and speech

We can choose to remain loving and constructive, both in thinking and speaking about others (1.Cor.13:5-7; 2.Cor.10:5; Eph. 4:29; 1. Pet.4:11). What God says always brings life; His words can heal and build us up, to encourage us and give us a fresh perspective. They are truthful and holy. This is an example for us. We can seek in others whatever is good, always believing that they acted with good intentions unless the opposite is plainly true. Even then, a kind word to carefully warn can work better than an accusation. Let's not ruin anyone's good name or accuse a person in the presence of others (Mt.18:15-20); but rather we should do whatever promotes building the person up in righteousness and getting their relationships and good name restored. It may help if we ask, "Lord, what are Your intentions for this person?". Think of his or her good qualities. God's plan for every person is uniquely beautiful! If we see such a person with an eye of faith and hope, this will fill our hearts and affect our prayers and attitude. (Col.3:8-15; Luk.6:45; Mat.15:18-19).

What we say is shaped by what we allow to enter our thoughts. Our thoughts even determine the condition of our heart and our emotions! These, in turn, determine our words and actions. Therefore, it is so important that we keep our thoughts clean and constructive, and that we ask the Lord to make us attentive to what enters our minds. Let God cleanse our thinking, as we ask His forgiveness and renewal (Rom.12:1-2).

The attitude of our heart will be visible in the way we speak about others. We know that we should not express our negative feelings about them, the only exception being the confidential conversation with a personal counselor. The letter of James has much to say about the sins of the tongue (Jam.1:14-27; 2:12-13; 3:2-18; 4:11-12; 5:9-12).

If we are often tempted to speak negatively about others, this may mean one of the following things:

(a) We still do not feel fully safe in the Lord and, therefore, we experience it as very painful when others seemingly harm us or do not accept us. It makes us not accept them either.

(b) We have not yet fully forgiven. In very deep wounds, it may be necessary to forgive almost daily in our heart and, often, new things may come up from our memory that we need to forgive. Therefore, we can ask God to give us His love for the one involved (Rom.5:5). We are all on the same level before God: kneeling level. We all need His forgiveness, and one day every knee shall bow before Him. (Is.45:23; Rom.14:11; Php.2:10)

(c) We are wrestling with a problem and have not been able to resolve it - but we are to try! It is important that we find out what exactly this problem is. Perhaps we have a distrust of others from a wound in our past - or a disturbed relationship with the person we tend to talk about. Finding the cause is a key issue in restoring such relationships (see Ch.8(9) below).

Finally: Accept no slander by others in your presence. It influences our opinion of others, creeping into the crevices of our heart where its influence will be hard for us to trace. The Book of Proverbs has much good advice on this. (Prov.4:23; 11:13; 12:18-20; 17:9; 18:8; 22:11; 25:9-12)

8.9 Solving difficult problems in relationships

What can we do if some relationships really do not seem to work? If the other person dislikes us and our friendly approach does not help at all, especially if some difficult event or situation has occurred, we may need to *confront* the person involved (see also Ch.2(8)). This is not easy but may be very necessary! As we do so, we can keep the following points in mind.

A. *First of all, again, be prepared to fully forgive.* Beforehand, pray about such a conversation very carefully, and ask the Lord for His help and wisdom in every step. We tend to avoid those we have a problem with, and the other person may want to avoid us! Therefore, it is good to ask the Lord for courage and for a speedy opportunity to speak with the one concerned. The longer we refrain from speaking, the more tension can build up inside us, making things harder for ourselves and for the other person. If it is difficult to meet him or her on some ordinary occasion, it may be necessary to make an appointment. If there is a major conflict with legal aspects to it, get advice on the practical side, first. Moreover, we can ask a trusted Christian counselor for advice. Even if there are no legal matters involved, we can still ask a counselor or a friend whom we trust to stand with us in prayer, yet avoiding any slander: "I have a very difficult conversation this Friday; please remember to pray for me".

If we are prepared to deal with any sin in our own life, we can approach the other person with upright heads and in openness, because God helps us in the fight! That way, the accuser will not be given a foothold in our life, and the criticism of others can even help us to find the weak spots in our armor and make us strong. The truth will set us, and them, free (Jhn.8:32; 1.Jhn.1:7; Hebr.12:11).

B. *Approach the person after prayer.* Learning to confront the situation and the person(s) involved is a crucial part of getting a problem solved. In my opinion, this is one of the most difficult steps we ever have to make in our Christian walk - yet if we never speak out how we feel, the problem remains. Speaking up may cost us a lot of courage, but both our relationships and our own peace of heart are worth it! Do we care enough to take this risk? We can go to him or her openly to talk things over, even though not everything in the situation may be quite clear yet. Let's not shy away from the person (except if we fear that he or she would harm us emotionally or physically). Do not wait for others to come to you, but go yourself as soon as the situation allows it (Matthew 5:23-24 even speaks about a situation where the other person has something against *us*, even though we may have nothing against them). It is not always easy to approach others, but it can be so effective. The sooner we do this, the better (Eph.4:26)!

C. *Be friendly as you speak, without accusations.* Just tell them about your own hurt feelings, asking them to help. Our vulnerable approach and openness make us less of a threat; we can "disarm" them, and thus make it easier for them to talk to us and in the end develop a relationship with us. Many people respond from their own wounded feelings, and if that comes out in the conversation we do not always need to take it personally. Such a wounded person may well behave towards others just as he or she behaves towards you. That helps us to forgive them, too.

Still, let us make *quite clear* whatever has hurt us. If the person listens, a first step to restoration may be there. In a major conflict, for instance if someone has clearly sinned against you, tell them also about the consequences (such as: you will go to the pastor, or to the police). Let them know how much you would like them to help resolve the matter. If the other person is unwilling, do not push your opinion at length but keep praying.

Sometimes, the best communication comes in normal conversation, also if we meet someone unprepared and thus have not been worrying about what to say! If the attitude of our heart was right towards him or her, this will then manifest itself. It is the good will that counts, not so much the remains of some hurting feelings - we can learn to handle those. As Christians, we learn to *act out of our convictions, not out of our feelings...*

D. *Seek the help of a trusted leader* if all else fails. Do not make a matter public but keep it confidential as much as you are able to. A leader can mediate between the other person and yourself, can talk things over less emotionally, and may do so at first without your presence. This can be very important for the restoration of the relationship and of the integrity of both parties. Let us do our utmost not to destroy someone's good name, however much we were right in the conflict. That will have a negative influence on our Christian example and their opinion of Christians, and make it much more difficult to restore the relationship.

E. *If no progress is made*, and the other person will not (or not fully) change his or her attitude, the conflict has not yet been resolved. If a private conversation does not help at all, or even makes things worse, or if a conversation is impossible to arrange because the other person is unwilling, then it is right to ask a pastor or elder in the church for advice. They can accompany us to talk things over with such a person (Mt.18:15-17). In legal issues, special advice may be needed from a lawyer, preferably a Christian (1.Cor.6:1-7). Moreover, it is very helpful to have trustworthy friends who pray for us and for all those involved.

Perhaps nothing has worked out whatever we attempted. That will be difficult, but we need to keep praying for the other person and do all that we can to improve things and to keep peace with them, in as far as it depends on us (Prov.25:15; Hebr.12:14; Eph.4:1-3; Col.3:13). Whatever the circumstances, we always need to do our best to love others and to be patient with them. That lesson will last a lifetime - a lesson of growing towards unity, in spite of all human differences.

F. *A thing to avoid: writing negative or warning letters.* There may be only a very few instances where a letter is needed, and then it is best to lovingly and prayerfully write it, asking that this letter be read by a trusted counselor before sending it off. The letters in the New Testament start with encouragements, even though there were many things wrong in the early church and people needed to be warned - still those Biblical letters were the fruit of an already existing relationship and mutual trust, written with much prayer and respect of what God had already done in the recipients.

However well-intended our letters are, the reader cannot pick up our good intentions from our voice and facial expression - and the letter may come across much more heavily than we intended. Moreover, long after the issue has been resolved, that piece of paper still exists and may rip open old wounds when it reappears! God may not be able to work through a letter if the other person feels threatened by it - he cannot truly receive the message. The Holy Spirit is the One Who convicts; not our letters. As someone who easily writes things down, I had to learn this the hard way and hope that readers will benefit from this advice.

8.10 Let God choose your relationships

Communication is the secret of good relationships

Before her wedding, a lady I know asked what the secret of a good marriage really was - she got the answer: "Communication"! We may learn to respectfully think of and speak to others and to become interested in them. Improving our communication with others is something we can learn; it helps us to understand them and to prevent problems. We can all practice it in daily life, at work or at home in the family. We do not need to share other people's opinions to love them and be their friends, but it helps to find out what they truly think and what points we have in common with them, even if our opinions differ in other matters. In the family, we can learn to lovingly treat one another and still be open and honest about difficult issues. We can also help children to develop their own opinion by our interest and respect, and by giving of our time to discuss all aspects of a matter. An open and loving atmosphere is something we can build up and pray for; it prepares children for times when they, too, may have to approach others in openness on difficult issues without hiding their own opinion.

There may be no one on earth with exactly the same opinion as we have, but we can still have many friends. It is especially the ones with "differing opinions" that we can learn from so much! That way, we can put ourselves to the test, and their opinions may have something essential to add to our life.

Keeping the lines open

When relationships with others are difficult, we can try to keep the normal communication channels open, by greeting them in a friendly manner while blessing them in our heart. Don't avoid them if you can – they could take this to be a lack of love. Pray for opportunities to make some natural conversation, such as about the weather, or offer your help when they need it. Be sensitive in how far you can go and if he or she is open. If a relationship does not seem to work, it may improve the situation if you ask the other person for help or advice, for a "favor". This may seem strange, but it often works! I wish you would try this (unknown to us, they may feel disliked by us). That person then can control the situation, which makes him or her less defensive - and you have a reason to give them some nice flowers afterwards - preferably delivering them yourself. If we faithfully water the tiny plants of friendship, which hesitantly try to bud, they may grow strong in the time ahead.

If a relationship is restored, this does not always mean that a deep friendship results soon. We do not need to blame ourselves for that! Some people think along different lines, have quite other hobbies or opinions. Let's respect them in that - they may have discovered truths that are still hidden from us, or had to live through experiences we are not aware of. After all, we can always "agree to disagree" on an issue.

We can ask God to bring permanent relationships and true friends on the path that He intends for us, with whom we can spend extra time, and to whom we may be of extra help as we rely on Him. Can we truly let God do the choosing? Let's openly approach all people, opening the door of our heart for them, asking the Lord to bring those who need us. Sometimes, people we never appreciated can become our very best friends, because during our battles together we have seen something of their heart!

8.11 Becoming a peacemaker

In your attitude to others, always choose to do what is good, allowing no bitterness to enter. If you have difficulties in relating to others, always give the Lord Jesus access to your feelings. As a child of God, He wants to make you a peacemaker (Mt.5:9). Forgiveness and prayer are the most important building blocks of the way to peace. Problems will pass, but *our choices of today determine our attitude of tomorrow and our feelings in days to come!* (Ch.5(3)) They are crucial for the development of our character and our future. Our choices in the past influence the way we handle relationships today, and perhaps we have to reconsider some of those choices. Do we look down on those of lesser standing? Or we may think, "That person is not my type". How did we come to such a negative thought? Were you disappointed by that person or by similar people in the past, and did you forgive them? As we have seen, forgiveness is the most important tool in healing both our relationships and ourselves.

It helps a lot if we ourselves become easier for others to deal with. We can use the time when things go well in relationships to keep building at these relationships, so that a good foundation is laid, and the relationship becomes better equipped for bad times that may come. It also helps to write down some of the good qualities you see in people you appreciate for their quality relationships, and to practically learn from their example. Finally, it also helps to write down, in what way you would like to be treated yourself and to start doing that for others, too, as the "Golden Rule" says (Mt.7:12).

Finally, we can work at having an inner attitude focused on the well-being of others, in unselfishness (Ro.15:1-7). That means: to serve others, being a blessing to them - also in practical areas. This will cost us something, but teaches us a lot about relationships. Let your actions not stem from flattering, but from a true wish to bless the other person. We can *choose* to do so, praying for it. Over time, something in our heart will change! Others feel whether our motives are pure and can then give us their trust more easily. It may also help them if, now and then, we show them some of our own weaknesses (Php.2:7) and where needed confess our sins. That makes it easier for them, too, to lay aside their battle dress and openly show us some of their hurts or problems. Then, we may be able to pray with them and possibly help them from our own experience. Real heart-to-heart contact - it is God's goal for our relationships!

9
LONGING FOR RENEWAL

Can we indeed change into the image of Jesus? That is so, for this is God's intention for us (2.Cor.3:16-18; 4:6-7; 5:17; Rom.8:29; 13:14; Eph.4:22-24; Col.3:10; Jhn.17:22,24) Our heavenly Father desires to have fellowship with us, as in the time before Adam and Eve fell into sin. If we want to grow closer to Him, we need renewal – and that is possible for all of us. We cannot do it in our own strength. No methods or laws can achieve this, but with God's help and power we can let Him work this out in us as we open our hearts to Him, invite Him in, and spend time with Him.

Most of us know that our victory is in the forgiveness of our sins, in a heart that Jesus has cleansed and filled with His peace. Jesus made this possible by suffering and dying in our place - by taking our punishment from us, for all the sins that we brought to Him. This is the foundation of our peace. How do we build on that, from the "new life" now yielded to His presence (1.Cor.3:9-16)?

Firstly, the Lord Jesus who now fills our hearts wants to work through us. We were once full of ourselves; now, we are full of Him! Moreover, we can pray and ask Him to fill us with the *mighty power of His Holy Spirit*, because we need His strength to testify to others. For this reason, God wants us to receive more of the Holy Spirit, and this is something we can all pray for as we look up to Him.

Secondly, it is very important that God receives more and more room in our hearts, as we spend time with Him. In our busy modern age, this is a constant battle. Here, we can also learn to grow in obedience. We may then find that He can reveal even more of His will to us. A very important passage here is Romans 12:1-2. There we find a true key - we are *changed by the renewal of our mind*!

The four keys to renewal are:
- A heart cleansed daily by Jesus, yielded to Him in love; (Rev.2:4)
- A desire to grow in obedience; (Jhn.14:21-26)
- A life filled with the Holy Spirit and prepared to share His truth; (Ac.1:8)
- A mind in the process of renewal by the Word of God. (Rom.12:1-2)

Many books were written on the first three keys, so in this chapter we will now focus on the fourth. *How can we have a renewed mind?*

9.1 Learning to be aware of our thoughts

How well I remember cycling through the Dutch city of Arnhem, thinking of the possibility of sinning in our thoughts. Nobody would see it. Obviously, you could sin in deeds or words - plain for all to notice - yet thoughts, however invisible, were clearly visible to God! (Hebr.4:12-13) As I pondered upon my bike, I could reach just one solution: from now on, I would check each thought on its purity, like putting a "policeman" next to it! However, I did waver a bit - was this too extreme? Or had I found an important key? I was struggling with legalism in those days and had not yet learned, that it would be better to ask the Lord Jesus to check my thoughts (a discovery I made at a later stage); but I did realize that it was necessary to ask Him to forgive me for "sinful thoughts". As I could find no other solution, this is what I decided to do. So the start was made - a tiresome undertaking. For in my head thoughts come and go, like the people in a crowded railway station, or like the many ingredients in a busy hotel kitchen. What had I gotten myself into?

However, after a few months, that decision had turned into a quiet habit, one that indeed brought a radical change and renewal in my life - and I have never regretted it since!

Our thought life is the source of our actions; there we interpret things that happen around us. It's in our mind that we make preparations and decisions; it is there that our character and future are in the making. It is there, however incredible, that even our feelings can be moulded (Ch.5(3,5)).

Thus, our thoughts are, as it were, the "kitchen", the feeding ground for our life. All sorts of things are prepared there; and it is there that the enemy hinders our efforts by accusing us, and it is there that we even accuse ourselves. However, the Bible says that we are to prove everything and *keep that which is good* (1.Thess.5:21-22; Gal.6:3-4). By doing this, I gradually learned not to accept everything that came into my thoughts, but to check it, make it "captive to obey Christ" (2.Cor.10:5; Ps.19:14), as we shall see how.

Our thought life, the very source of our actions, often escapes our scrutiny - no one notices anyway, and who would care? Often some distrustful, or unclean or fearful thoughts and expectations enter our minds; thoughts that can turn around the truth or even excuse the evil around us when we feel this is to our advantage. However, the Bible has much to say about our thought life (Ps.139:21-24; Mt.15:18-20; Eph.4:17-24; Hebr.4:12). As I started to get serious about my thoughts, it was difficult in the beginning to bring so many thoughts that had grown into deformed patterns and sinful habits throughout the years into God's presence, to ask for His forgiveness and healing!

The kitchen of our thoughts

It seems easier to work with what the eye can see: the good impression we want to make before others by acting a certain way - for others do not see what we think. However, God sees it, and much of it is useless or even sinful! What is the kitchen of your thoughts like - are there dirty pictures on the wall? If so, you may lose concentration while you cook. Is it a filthy place? The quality of what you dish up will suffer, and it can even be hazardous to the health. Are the ingredients greed, ambition, or unbelief? That makes cooking a burden rather than a pleasure. What recipe do we cook, "Love for the Lord", "blessing others" or "selfishness"? Perhaps we use herbs of bitterness, jealousy or hatred; then there is a nasty atmosphere in the kitchen and creativity is gone. Or, perhaps, an overly strict discipline reigns in the kitchen, a painful legalism that leaves no energy for happy creativity? True perfection lies in just being with Jesus and reflecting His holiness, not making up one of our own... In our limited human strength, we cannot create good order in our thoughts; but we can ask the Lord Jesus to come into our thought life and hand over the government of our thoughts to Him. Then, the "thought kitchen" can become a place cleansed by Him; a place where it is good to be, where creativity comes forth and good things are prepared to bless others. God longs for our thoughts to produce good things, spreading an odour that pleases Him (praise, fellowship with Him), food for the repair and refreshment of our own lives as well as for the spiritual hunger of those around us. May the ingredients of our work be the fruit of the Holy Spirit: love, joy, peace, patience... (Gal.5:22-23).

9.2 Thoughts cleansed by God

What can we do with, for instance, unclean thoughts? (Ch.9(3) & App.3) We cannot clean the "kitchen of our thoughts" ourselves – however often we may have tried. What we can do is to allow the Lord Jesus to come in each time and to ask Him to forgive the sinful thoughts that we have allowed in, and to let Him reign again over our "thought kitchen". He wants to forgive us these thoughts and to cleanse us from all unrighteousness (1.Jhn.1:9), and so He gives us a sound basis for a renewed thought life. He understands, too, from what weakness we acted, as well as where we acted irresponsibly. A good touchstone for our thoughts is Php.4:8, a passage helpful to learn by heart. Acting just from this Scripture can already be strategic for the renewal of our thoughts and indeed for our life. It also shows us the character of the Lord Jesus and His thoughts about us! (Jer.29:11, Is.55:7-13).

Another quite important step to renewal is to be *sure* that your sins are forgiven. Do you really know that, even today? Do you bring new sins to the Lord Jesus as soon as you detect them? It is so important to truly receive His forgiveness for ourselves and remember: God *has* forgiven me, it is in His Word! It has a deep and healing influence on our thoughts and feelings to know that we have been washed by the blood of the Lamb. God *totally* forgives us because of Jesus' sacrifice; He does not remember it any more (Col.1:12-14; Rom.4:5-7; Ac.13:38-39; Mk.2:10). Therefore, we may truly think of ourselves as "washed clean" - or do we see ourselves still through those old spectacles? Here, too, obedience is so important in our thoughts. The "kitchen of our thoughts" is now clean - and we can then ask the Holy Spirit to fill it with His fragrance as well as with His power to help us in all we do. Now that Jesus has forgiven us, there is no more condemnation; we are "in Christ" through that open relationship with Him, and a "new creation". What a glorious thing to know! (Rom.8:1-2; 2.Cor.5:17; Jhn.14:20-21; 2.Tim.4:8).

In Christ Jesus, we now have a new foundation for our life - a life together with God. Whenever we stumble into sin, we may know that by asking His forgiveness we can get up, grasp His hand (He even reaches out for us!), and continue to walk with Him. May our hearts always be open to God the Father Who loves us and is ready to meet us as we pray from a cleansed heart (Ps.51:10). That way, we remain "in Christ", as a branch on the Vine (Jhn.15:3-6). The sanctification that the Bibles speaks about so frequently is: having our sins washed away as soon as we notice them, and a growing love for the Lord (1.Cor.1:27-31; Jer.31:33-34). He wants to give us a "new heart" and fill us with His Holy Spirit for the power that we need to fulfil His calling upon our lives (Ac.1:8; 4:29-31; Rom.11:29; Gal.5:16-18,22-25; Php.3:13-14; 2.Thess.1:11; 2.Tim.1:9; 2.Pet.1:10).

Through the forgiveness of our confessed sins, the Lord Jesus restores our relationship with God so that it can grow deeper and more intimate. Do we stop at having received forgiveness, or do we continue on the path towards the heavenly Father, now that Jesus has opened this way up to us? This is why He came…

9.3 How to bring our thoughts under the government of Jesus

As we find in 2.Cor.10:5, we can bring our thoughts under the authority of Christ, as we decide to obey only Him. We may be very pessimistic about our thought life, but God in His goodness and loving mercy has prepared a solution! Obedience in our thinking comes not by our own tiresome efforts, but by asking the Holy Spirit to help us and to fill our thoughts as we hold on to Jesus. In the past, having discovered that we can sin in our thoughts, I took the step of dedicating my thought life to God (see Ch. 9(1)). It taught me, that I am responsible for whatever I allow to enter my thoughts - and that proved a real blessing, preparing in me more depth, stability and victory. Some good Scriptures to read are 1.Chron.28:9; Prov.23:7; Php.4:8-9; Ps.94:19; 139:23; Prov.16:3.

We may not necessarily have allowed every passing thought to enter our mind. Make sure you deal with uninvited guests! In the kitchen of our thoughts, only those are allowed in that are welcome in the Lord's presence - He now reigns there, and only good ingredients are wholesome. It has often been said that we are not responsible if birds fly around our head, but we are responsible indeed if we let them build a nest upon our head (allowing wrong thoughts to enter, and fantasizing with them). So: if a wrong thought comes, we are responsible for dealing with it! Put wrong ingredients that somehow entered your kitchen in the trash outside your kitchen door. If you have consciously let them in, just ask God to forgive you. Then, stop thinking about it by focusing on the good ingredients and on the work at hand, as a good cook would!

Where do thoughts come from?

Even as a child, I wondered where thoughts came from. Our brain works in a complicated way, and I understand little about that. But in practice, I found the following categories:

A. *Thoughts that seem to come up "by themselves"* and apparently without reason (these may have come up out of myself, from God, or from the enemy of our souls) - things that I have not consciously been thinking up or allowed in. This can, for example, be a wrong thought that I cannot remember as being part of my previous thought life (it's not from my own kitchen cupboard), or an impression like a dove that flies into my kitchen window. I have not ordered these ingredients myself for my "thought kitchen", and may freely send them back - unless they are good and useful, or even a gift from the heavenly Father! I am not responsible for any thought ingredients that I have not ordered, unless I accept them and start using them.

As soon as we find any bad thought ingredients, we must immediately distance ourselves from these and send them back - otherwise, they will ruin our recipe and the results of our work. From the thoughts that are useful, we choose those that we need to work with. It may take some time before we get used to thinking selectively upon what is good, but we can hold on to Jesus and ask Him to help us in our "kitchen of thoughts". It is wonderful to know that we may choose what we allow to enter, and what we may throw out into the trash outside our kitchen door! (By the way, do you know of any cook who spends all his time on worrying about the trash outside, rather than on the lovely ingredients and recipes at hand? It's not even fun.)

Perhaps we have often prayed for God's guidance as we seek Hiis goal for our life. Our thoughts, too, belong to this. Are we open to only thinking upon what pleases Him? It can become a firm decision inside of us: I choose to only allow those thoughts in that God appreciates, those that are pure and constructive. Fighting against sinful thoughts, however, never helped me; but it did help to focus on *other* and better thoughts or to start doing something constructive (like shopping, cleaning, etc.). Should wrong thoughts keep coming, then it can help to ask for God's forgiveness and to hand our thought life over to Him. For instance, we can pray, "Lord, I want to ask You to form my thoughts anew; today I hand over my thought life to You afresh" (Rom.12:1-2).

At times, it may seem as if the enemy gives us certain thoughts. We may simply put them with the trash, and reprimand the enemy by saying: "go away, Satan, I belong to Jesus and He lives and reigns within my heart!" The enemy does not like to be with Jesus. Then, you will notice that such thoughts will start losing their power over you. So be persistent: before the name of Jesus, Satan must flee. How lovely that Jesus wants to reign in the "kitchen of our thoughts" and that He helps us clean up any mess still left there!

B. *Things that come up from our memories and feelings* - that is, from past experiences and things that we are at least partly conscious of. Our interpretation of past events may not always have been right and sometimes even sinful - we bear part of the responsibility for this. In such cases, I can ask the Lord to show me where I acted or interpreted wrongly. Perhaps I misjudged people in such a situation or did not forgive them; then, I am still entangled in the situation and have not become detached from it (Mt.7:1-5; Mk.11:25-26). Things can work like this: You meet a person and think, "what an unpleasant man, he reminds me of my old enemy Jim" (we are biased); or, "There we have John again, he is always against me" (which may not be true at all). The solution is then: to forgive Jim and John their old sins, so that we can more objectively judge both them and others around us who remind us of them. Then we also learn to approach them without prejudice and even to establish a relationship with them, without comparing them to others who have hurt us in the past. Forgiveness is such a mighty weapon! God also wants to forgive our biases and wrong attitudes. It is only through the blood of Christ that we can have the kitchen of our heart cleansed of bitterness, fear, and prejudice. How little do we sometimes know about the motives of others - God knows, and yet He still loves them. We can choose to learn that, too. Loving comes firstly by a continual choice of your heart; emotions may only come much later...

C. *Things that I "think up myself" consciously*; with thought-ingredients that I willingly made or admitted myself, and that I work with in the kitchen of my thoughts and heart.

Many of these can be quite all right and even necessary, like much of what is already there in my memory (through family, school, library, TV, friends, and events). For such ingredients, I do bear a responsibility. I have kept them, cook them up, work with them daily; and they deeply influence my life, my work, and my feelings. It is important to sort out any bad ingredients and to do away with them, as I bear responsibility for what I have admitted into my thoughts in the past. I am free to stop allowing wrong thought-ingredients any space in my kitchen - not by pushing them to the back of the cupboard (they will still occupy a hidden space there and start to stink!), but by looking at them closely and firmly kicking them out! I can do so by asking God to forgive me, and by turning my back on these thoughts when they do not meet the test of God's standards in the Bible.

As you try to kick wrong thoughts out, you may find that some thought-ingredients are quite "sticky"! You have thought about them for such a long time that they have become almost habitual - it is then good to clearly oppose them with the truth: "I have forgiven Peter and John now. God has forgiven me for these bad thoughts". This is especially true for thoughts in the sexual realm (App.3), and it is no small danger to read dubious books or watch wrong TV-programmes. You are simply heaping up bad ingredients in the cupboards of your thought-kitchen! That storing room can then no longer be filled with good and pure ingredients. What are we doing with our life? It is reflected by what we have stored over the years in these cupboards of our thoughts. They may be so full of rubbish that it is a challenge to fill the remainder with things that are lovely and pleasant before God. As we have seen, Philippians 4:8 is an important key here. As we direct our thoughts to whatever is pure and lovely, this has a healing effect on our soul. We then have less opportunity to occupy our thoughts with uncleanness or bitterness. This does not mean that we close our eyes to all that happens in the world or that we should not look at news programmes. As long as we can keep our thoughts clean, it is not wrong to know something of the stressful times in which we live, and in which we can become salt and light. We can pray for difficult situations in the world, yet not be so occupied with its sinfulness that it makes us gloomy! We can find an inner balance and joy in the Lord, in spite of the needs around us - only then can we hand out to others from the good things He gives to us.

9.4 Check whether your thoughts are true

It is important to see whether our old ways of looking at things are untrue, and to exchange them for the way God sees things (we find them in the Bible). We can learn this by choosing to do so again and again, and by getting to know His Word more intimately. In the beginning, this seems no small task; but if we love the Lord and remain close to Him, we will come to love His opinion and will ask Him into the kitchen of our thoughts to help us remove what needs to be replaced by His loving hand.

We may think something to be true about ourselves or others, whereas these thoughts are based on (mostly damaged and thereby untrustworthy) feelings and emotions. This was true in my own life - I simply "felt" things that way and did not seem able to break out of this pattern and see the objective truth of God's Word as being "for me, too". My thought-life was approximately as follows:

MY FEELINGS → MY THOUGHTS → GOD'S WORD

I was guided by my feelings, which were untrustworthy due to sin and past hurts, as a measuring rod to interpret what happened around me. These feelings told me things that I regarded as true in my thoughts. God's Word came last of all, and often did not fit in with my own impressions. I then found it hard to believe God. That way, my wounded feelings dominated my thoughts, which then did not seem to fit in with God's Word where I read about God's love, power, and hope. Strangely enough, it was a real discovery to me that God's truth is higher than mine (Is.55:7-9)! I had to truly accept this in practice, as a fact, when my thoughts in any situation differed from His. My feelings would be: "This situation is hopeless, it will never turn into anything good" - and my thoughts would hold that to be true! Yet

God's Word says, "I know the thoughts I have towards you, thoughts of peace and not evil, to give you a future and a hope" (Jer.29:11). Did I choose to stick to my own gloomy thoughts, thoughts that were a lie? Strangely enough, I found it hard to exchange my old home-made lies for the beautiful truth of God, and had to choose for His truth again and again until it sank in. Finally, I decided to no longer give my feelings the supremacy but only the Word of God - and this meant a *breakthrough*! This is shown below:

GOD'S WORD → MY THOUGHTS → MY FEELINGS

God's Word received the highest place; after that came my thoughts and intellect with which I understood and held on to His truth, imprinting these onto my soul like David did (Ps.42:5,11; 103), so that after some time my feelings would also come in line with the facts God had shown.*)

Let's remember that person, of whom we thought, "What an unpleasant man, he reminds me of Jim". If that would now happen to me, I would be prone to think, "God loves that man but I do not even know him; and what is there about Jim that I have not forgiven him? Is there anyone else he reminds me of whom I have not forgiven?" That way, we can check our thoughts against God's truth; and our thoughts, in turn, can affect our feelings to bring these in line with His goodness and love (Ch.5(3)).

Of course, this does not mean that we throw all our own thoughts out of the window. There are enough objective truths around us that we may take into account. We can learn lessons from nature and in school, from true events, or from experiences with truly sinful people. However, let us ask the Lord to help us receive His light in any situation we wrestle with.

Therefore, do not accept any lies about yourself and others, even though your feelings cannot help you because of old interpretations of past events. Your father may have failed you, but that does not mean he always did, nor that all men will fail you. God asks us to forgive others just like He forgave us (Eph.4:32; Mt.6:12-15). His truthful plan for us is and remains good forever (Ps.40:18; 91:14-16; 139:16-17), whatever our feelings say.

If we keep holding on to old lies because we rely on our feelings rather than on God's Word, the enemy can find a back door in these lies to enter our life with his destructive work. Just think of how you developed negative thoughts about yourself as a child. Perhaps those who had authority over you (such as a parent or teacher) said in an angry moment, "Nothing will become of you" - have you started to believe that lie? Did it become part of your thoughts and feelings? It may be of help to consider what kind of lies we have admitted (firstly about ourselves, but also about others, about God, about the world at large). Such wrong thoughts tend to sink into your feelings about yourself! What do these feelings tell you today; where are they contrary to what you (if you think objectively) know to be true about yourself - and what can you do about the difference?

A. Make a list of such feelings, asking the Lord to keep revealing these to you. Then, place the truth of God behind it. In my personal case, such a list would have looked like this:

My own untruthful feelings and thoughts	God's truth about me in the Bible
1 I feel less valuable than most other people; I often feel quite worthless.	God sees me as precious and honourable, He loves me. I'm certainly not less valuable than others, and there is only *one* of me! (Is.43:4; Jhn.3:16)
2 God is quite strict and hard to please. I cannot do anything right anyway.	God is love. He has come to give me an abundant life. He is pleased with His people and with me. (1.Jhn.4:7-12; Jhn.10:10-11; Eph.1:4-10; Luk.2:14)

B. *Ask God to forgive you for thoughts that were not based on truth*, and which make your life so difficult at times. Ask Him to help you recognize these and to replace them by His truth by a choice of your will, as soon as these thoughts return. It can help to learn any such Scripture verses that you wrote down by heart, so that you have the truthful "sword of the Spirit" (Eph.6:17) to fight such thoughts ready at hand. That way, we can counteract the attacks of the enemy who tries to pull us down into negativity.

C. *Ask the Lord what people and events played a role in your untruthful thoughts and negative feelings*, especially if they have been there for a long time (perhaps even since childhood). In my case, old problems with my overly strict father had caused much of my wrong thinking about myself - and I had not fully forgiven him. Perhaps your problems stem from a different source, but it does pay off to write down any causes you can find, and to consciously *start forgiving* the people involved for every deed and every painful detail that you still remember - especially for what hurt you most. It is an indispensable ingredient for the healing of your own soul!

It helps to keep forgiving as long as any pain or bitterness is felt when the memory comes up, or when later on we remember other hurtful details. The pain will then fade away, and we are able to truly forget, without pushing things away artificially. Dig those things up, take a good look at them, forgive all people involved thoroughly, and hand it over to God - and it will leave your life...

D. *Take some extra time and opportunity to exercise your new thoughts.* During a prayer meeting I once shared how hard I found it to believe in the goodness of God (more on this in Ch.5(3)). My brain knew it from the Bible, but my feelings didn't acknowledge it. An otherwise shy young man put me on the spot by saying: "Clara, you believe a lie!" What a shock that was... for I had to admit it was true. My feelings believed in an inaccessible and difficult Authority, not in a loving heavenly Father. I decided to do something about it there and then - to impregnate as it were my whole being with the truth of God's goodness, continually thanking Him for His loving character: that He created me and wanted to make something good out of my life. Furthermore, I asked forgiveness for the fact that I had harboured a lie about Him deep inside. As I went through the day (on a walk, while doing dishes, etc.) I kept praising Him for His goodness - and I did this for many days, *even though at that moment I did not feel anything*. I just kept confessing the truth and dismissing the lies. David spoke to his soul (Ps.42:5,11; 43:5), and so may we. The feelings about God and myself, that I had harboured for such a long time in the past by thinking wrongly, were slower to pick up the truth than my brain; and it took just over one month for the truth to sink in until also my feelings responded to it. However – my feelings *did* change, the more I exercised truthful thinking. What a precious discovery that was.

9.5 *Taking time to enjoy God's love, to be with Him and to thank Him*

Even as very young Christians, we can thank Him, sing before Him, count our blessings, and keep praising Him for all His goodness, in spite of daily problems that we encounter (Eph.1:3, 5:20; 1.Thess.5:16-18; Hebr.13:15; Ps.139:17-18). The Lord Himself is the best thing that could ever happen to us! Just try it for a day - spend the whole day thanking Him for everything and sing before Him. It's like a bath of renewal in itself.

As we spend much time close to Him in the stillness, He can enlighten our heart with His love and glory and refreshing presence. As we look up to Him often, we start looking like Him more and more, even reflecting some of His glory (Ps.34:5; 2.Cor.3:18; 4:6-7).

As we direct ourselves more and more towards God, there is less and less space left for negative thoughts (Rom.12:21; Php.4:4-9). That wonderful hidden walk with God is for each of us (Ps.25:14-15) and we do not need to go to a convent for it! We all have a quiet room in our hearts that we carry with us always and that we can set apart for Him. Thus, we can silently and invisibly pray to Him during an important conversation, and thank Him during our work, as we drive a car, in the office or at home. That, in a true sense, is "walking with God". That way, too we use our thoughts for good: to love Him even with our minds (Mt.22:37).

9.6 Finding out Who God is from His Word

Reading the Bible frequently will help us to find out about God's character. If we just take the Psalms, so much is written there that helps us in our personal relationship with Him (Ps. 8, 23, 51, 62, 84, 91, 103, 116, 144, etc.). Moreover, reading in the Bible often is a most effective touchstone for our thoughts (Hebr.4:12; Deut.11:18-20; Josh.1:8). As we discover its truths with our mind, we can imprint them on our souls, so that even our feelings start to pick them up. Scriptures that we find difficult to practice or grasp can be learned by heart (e.g. 2.Cor.5:17). That is a beautiful way to imprint them on our soul, so that not just our mind but our whole being takes part in the renewal (Rom.12:2). It helps to learn by heart any verse that especially applies to your life, and to practice what it says. A great basis to start with can be to memorize Scriptures like Mt.5:3-12; Php.4:4-8, 1.Thess.5:14-24; Gal.5:22-25. As we follow these words, they can transform our life, even in trials.

As we read the Word, it can help to read a different translation for a change. It's meaning can then speak to us afresh. In all this, however, it is important that we actually obey what Gods Word shows us. Only if we do what He tells us, can renewal truly permeate our lives. Such full obedience will not always be easy, and it will often cost us a great deal. Nevertheless, as the seed of the Word falls into the fruitful soil of our hearts, it can bring forth much fruit (Mt.13:19-23; Jhn.12:24-25).

One day I discovered that every personal commission of God also includes a promise: the promise that it is possible to obey this commandment, because God also gives me the strength to fulfil it! That way, whatever God tells me becomes a tremendous challenge: "How is He going to work it out this time?" (Rom.7:18; Php.2:13).

9.7 Filled with God's Holy Spirit

For renewal, we can ask the Lord Jesus again and again to fill us with the Holy Spirit - not as a one-time experience, but as a lifestyle (Is.11:2-5; Mk.1:8; Jhn.14:26; Acts 1:8; Eph.1:17-18, 3:16-19, 4:23, 5:18-21). Therefore, it helps to regularly pray for this, for instance whenever we have brought our sins to Him and have received His forgiveness (many good and helpful books have been written on this subject). Moreover, if the Lord has given you some spiritual gifts, then do not forget to put these into practice (2.Tim.1:6-7), so that they can grow and bring forth fruit. It is the Holy Spirit Who fills us with wisdom, strength, and a sound mind, so that He can use us. We so much need the Holy Spirit if we want to grow closer to God, to let Him into our thought life and receive the "mind of Christ" (1.Cor.2:12-16; Php.2:5-9; Rom.8:26-29).

The Holy Spirit is connected with forgiveness and renewal, even in the Old Testament (e.g. Ps.51:11-13; Ezek.11:19-20). Throughout history, we have been able to see the crucial role that the Holy Spirit has in revival - and yet we tend to forget this in our own life. Often, we may try to produce the fruit of the Holy Spirit by ourselves and become frustrated by the fruitless results. However, the fruit that God longs to see comes by the Holy Spirit Whom He allows to live inside of us - not by our hard work. Therefore, we may reach out and ask Him for that infilling by the Holy Spirit, as we live in openness before the Lord in all that we do.

In our walk with the Lord, it is good to pay attention to the Holy Spirit. Then, we will not do things He dislikes and that could lead us into temptation (sin mostly starts in our thoughts): things like bad magazines, violence on TV, sex films, bars, or friends who draw us away from the Lord and who resist our testimony. We will have to let go - but what the Holy Spirit wants to give us is so endlessly rich! It can be so valuable to write down the new things that we learn and experience in a notebook; it will be an encouragement for the future, and these insights can become a help to others.

9.8 Thoughts lead to choices

The character we now have has, to an important extent, been shaped by the thoughts and choices we made in the past. The person we will be in the future depends not simply on our genes or events or choices of the past, but especially on the ongoing renewal of our mind (Rom.12:1-2) and the new choices that we are still going to make. What a hopeful prospect! Of course, our family traits and natural abilities also play a role (a person with musical talents would sooner decide to take piano lessons than those who don't). God has given all of us the ability to choose whatever is good, to love and help others. However, many of us are not entirely free to choose what they would want, due to shyness or a lack of love in the past. We then tend to focus on filling the painful gaps in our own life, on dressing our wounds, and may have little strength left to give anything to others. We often do not have a "grip" on these things, but may ask God to help us and fill us with His divine love and with the Holy Spirit, when we feel this is needed. The Lord is our Counsellor and holds our future in His hands; we can ask Him to come in, even in our thought life, to teach and guide us.

Our thought life is of crucial importance in our choices, and it is good to take time and find out what we really think. For instance: John passes by without greeting me - I think: doesn't he want to see me? - as a result I behave very coolly towards him when he asks me a question the next day. My thoughts have interpreted his silence as unfriendliness (perhaps John simply was immersed in his own thoughts and did not notice me). However, the choice I made was: I treat him the same way; or perhaps: I am hurting but he must not notice, so I behave as if I do not care about our friendship anyway - and all the time I hurt and, in the end, he does too. Much of this thinking may be almost subconscious (the more it becomes conscious, the more it seems to hurt). Therefore, it would be interesting to ask ourselves, "why did I behave like that? What choice, what thoughts lay behind that? Why do I have a problem with this, and since when? It helps to no longer push away such thoughts but write them down honestly and place them before the Lord: "What are

Your thoughts on this?" That gives direction to our thoughts - that they be honest and pure, not manipulating but taking courage to talk things over and to be truthful about our own weaknesses and opinions.

Our thoughts are hidden, and yet they have a strategic influence upon our life. They determine the direction we take towards the future! Therefore, it remains important that we ask the Lord to take part in our thinking and to guide us. The earlier in life we make a certain decision, the longer and deeper such a choice influences us - especially because our personality is formed at an early age, when we are influenced more deeply by the things around us and the childish way we interpret them. This is one reason why it is important to serve the Lord when we are young, as He then helps form our characters, laying a firm foundation for our life. But He can also help us in that later on in life! Our thoughts and choices of today will influence future events, as well as form our feelings and character. If we have a character weakness, He can help. He can also help if we continually feel hurt in certain instances. *What* are these instances, and *since when* do they hurt you - have you ever thought about that? It is an important key to change. The causes may be long ago, with a choice that was not a good one. Yet there is a road to healing! I remember how, as a teenager, I stood before the window after a severe disappointment, and said to myself, "I will no longer give real trust to anyone, for it hurts too much to get disappointed". That choice deeply influenced my relationships and interest in people. Many years later, when I remembered that, I asked God to forgive me for that bad choice, to forgive the person who hurt me back then, and made quite a different choice.

Forgiveness plays such an important part in all of this. I began to forgive all the others who had disappointed me in life as well. There was now room in my heart to make different choices: to esteem and appreciate them - in spite of their shortcomings. As I asked God to forgive me for closing my heart to people, He enlarged my heart so that it could truly open up to others, even to deep friendships. In forgiveness, God gives us the key to a renewed and different way of thinking about those around us: instead of holding on to bitterness and disappointment (an old choice to negatively esteem things and judge others) there is then room for gentleness and mercy - and that does a world of good, even to ourselves. So: we can really *do* something about it!

If we remain unforgiving, we limp on in the daily harness of our old unconscious choices that have sunk in so deeply. I remember a lady that had grown up in a very untidy home, and she was very ashamed of it. She could have chosen to think, "How terrible, we come from such a messy home, but it will probably never change - that's who we are". She would then have become like her parents. However, not knowing about the key of forgiveness, she made a different choice: Never would it happen to her! She grew up to become a painfully clean and neat lady, not a tiny speck of dust was allowed in her house. She swung to the other extreme and remained out of balance. Unconsciously, she had fallen prey to that different choice, which began to imprison her thoughts. It would have been better for her to forgive her parents. She would then have received the space to develop her own lifestyle, not guided by the past or having to fight it; as well as becoming open to her parents.

This principle also works in many other areas of life. What is it that we keep struggling with? By both extending forgiveness and receiving it from God, as well as forgiving ourselves (!), we grow in balance and stability. We can then find room for our own lifestyle, one that fits our personality and the thoughts that God has for our life. It is a space in which we can truly be "ourselves" and become the person God has intended us to be in His goodness.

9.9 Being a wholesome influence in our circumstances and environment

Our society often thinks and speaks destructively; we can refresh others by our truthful, pure, and merciful thinking that builds up and encourages other people. Scriptures to help us work this out practically are for example Philippians 4:4-9. Our attitude can then grow into a good influence on those around us and improve the atmosphere at home or at our work. It is especially worthwhile to guard our *speech*; Bible passages like 1.Peter 4:11 and James 1:19 & 26 are a special challenge. Being a good influence will cost less effort as we start learning to fill our mind with God's thoughts of love and forgiveness towards people, and as we learn to prayerfully build relationships. We need not be not afraid of asking non-Christians for forgiveness too, if we have sinned against them. I once got a friendship through it. (Luk.21:15; Mat.10:19-20, 12:35; Prov.16:23)

If people around you often make dirty jokes or ridicule and slander others, it will not be easy to work towards a good atmosphere or keep your own thoughts clean. Still, by our attitude we can show that we think differently; not so much by telling them (this often works counterproductively) but by not getting involved in the discussion or even by walking away from it (Ps.1:1). What we *can* do is promote the things that are good, protect the good name of others, help and encourage them, and show them love. That way, we act in the opposite spirit: towards whatever is pure and true and lovely (Php.4:8; Rom.12:21).

*) A more familiar version is the "Faith-Fact-Feeling" sequence (found e.g. in F.B. Meyers book "The Secret of Guidance", Moody Press, Ch.4). However, the version in this book: "God's Word-Thoughts-Feelings" seems easier to apply and at least as accurate.

APPENDIX

This appendix deals somewhat more deeply with the *guidelines* from the Introduction of this book. We can also use these guidelines as a starting theme during a Bible study or small group meeting, where one such guideline can be discussed with the help of some of the Scriptures mentioned below. To that end, some questions for discussion have been added that are not only a first step towards praying for people in the group, but that can also be useful for those who simply read these.

1 Stand in the "first love" to the Lord (Rev.2:4)

"First love" means that God is at the top of our priority list, that we spend time with Him and sit at His feet; that we strive to know and love Him above all else in our life, in real dedication and obedience (Jhn.14:21-23; Rom.8:28; 1.Jhn.2:15; 4:20-21: Mt.22:37-39). We were even *created* for His love! Seek His presence, being satisfied with nothing less. It is so important to take time for Him and walk with Him. The noise and pressures of life seem to drown the quiet times with Him, and yet we need that rest and refreshing presence of the Lord. Therefore, let's not lose sight of Him as the goal of our life, by earnestly guarding our relationship with Him. He wants the best for us, and we may always hold on to His love!

Moreover, that first love is also the most important step towards our inner healing and spiritual growth - a growing closer to Him as well as to our "neighbor" (Luk.10:27). In His presence, we receive comfort and rest. In His presence, we get the right perspective of our problems and circumstances; also, it is the first step towards a solution. From Him, too, we learn what true love is for ourselves and others (Jhn.13:34-

35). Do we really believe this, or do we keep looking at circumstances and people?

What can we do when we lost that "first love" for the Lord Jesus?

A. Ask the Lord to forgive you, and accept His forgiveness with all your heart. This is a serious situation (Rev.2:5) that we need to make our first priority!

B. Yield your life to God afresh, and give Him the keys of your heart and its desires.

C. Spend time with Him daily, working consciously at the renewal of your love relationship with Him. It is important to seek Him and spend time to enjoy His presence, even without special prayer requests - just focusing on placing Him first in your life, in full obedience (Hebr.12:1-13; Jhn.14:6,15,21,23). It is when we look at Him as the goal of our existence that He can make a straight path for our feet - for He Himself is the way, the truth and the life. If we lose sight of Him, we lose sight of the way and go our own. That can happen so easily, even when we are busy for the Lord! Can He still guide us with His eyes? (Ps.16:8-11; 32:8-9).

D. Find out what has distracted you from spending time at His feet, and what has taken His place of priority away. What idol has taken the throne of your life? Was it a busy lifestyle, some frustration, a commandment you did not like to keep, or the love of prestige and money? They are the *wrong goals*... Make Him your only goal once again, and ask Him to fill you with His love. There is no alternative in Gods kingdom. You will discover that He is more than worth it!

Perhaps we feel that serving God will cost us too much. What exactly is that thing that we could lose? It may well be something we need to lay on the open palm of our hands, for God to take away or leave as He pleases. Let's not forget that He is such a good God! He truly loves us. We may realize that people will often disappoint us, but not God. We often think, "if only I had this...", "if only that were different"... not realizing that the true solution and our happiness do not lie there: for after solving one problem, so many other imperfect things can come to the forefront to make us sad. What do we focus on: on all the problems around us, or on our true Friend and Helper? That is an ongoing choice. True happiness comes from the Lord Jesus, from the love and friendship He gives, as the highest and only true Goal there is. He wants to be with us always (Matt.28:20). It is so good to know that and to spend time with Him often, satisfied in being dependent on Him. He gives us rest and joy (Mt.11:28-30; Ps.16:8-9; 23:2). Being with Him will make us stronger even in difficult circumstances and changes things from within.

Group discussion and prayer:
1. Do you know from experience what the "first love to the Lord" means? Can you tell something about it, or about experiencing His presence?
2. Have you sometimes lost contact with God, and what caused it? What do you think can be done in such situations?
3. Have you come closer to the Lord during the past months? Are there some people who want prayer for this?

2 Maintain a living prayer relationship with Him

We can focus on having a prayer relationship as natural as breathing, in other words: to do all things prayerfully, discussing them with the Lord (1.Thess.5:17; Eph.6:18). If He is our "first love", this will become the natural thing for us to do. We may discuss the small and big decisions of the day with Him, and pray for the people we work with. We can, for instance, pray before talking to someone or (during a difficult situation) quickly and silently pray with open eyes. We can ask for His guidance when we need to make a decision, His advice in buying new glasses. We can silently pray for His blessing on those we see around us, for forgiveness for a sinful thought, His love for a difficult client, His wisdom in spending our time. Throughout the day, we can keep in contact with our heavenly Father, the King over all! He is a Helper in need, and looks forward to meeting with us as we pray. Also, He is the one teaching us to pray (Mat.6:5-15).

In our busy lives, it is less hard to find a good time to set apart for Bible reading and prayer when we have made this our priority. What do we spend our time on? Of course, it is good to bring all the "big issues of our life" to the Lord and spend more time with Him when we need His answer; but also in the small events of every day, His guidance can play an important part. This is what it means to "walk with the Lord", by the guidance that He gives. For some, it is best to pray for this at the beginning of the day - between the hustle and bustle of our daily work there may be no time for that - but we can draw on Him for strength and wisdom whenever we need it (Ps.37:3-5). Moreover, we live in a very needy world that needs our intercession, whatever time of day it is.

It can be very helpful to look up Bible passages on prayer that we find in a Concordance, or to read some good books about it. What is helpful, what could we use in our situation? We can find our own practical way to pray, as a friend of mine discovered. She asks the Lord what He wants her to pray for, how long she should pray for it (this can be up to several hours, which she may divide over the week), and then she faithfully prays. She does this, for instance, walking alone in a nearby park, or simply in her home, while praying both with her mind and in tongues (the prayer language that God gave her). This has become a source of strength both to her and to those for whom she prays.

Another friend who loves to pray does this while, for instance, cleaning out a cupboard on a quiet afternoon. This dull task becomes interesting as she brings the needs of God's people before His throne. We can pray in our car, behind our desk, in the kitchen. Our style to pray is not as important as our relationship with Him. He is the Source, He is the Fulfilment. He knows.

A *prayer group* can be of help in learning how to pray. I once belonged to such a group, where we met with a few friends every week. We would look at the news on TV, write down the prayer topics (including our own), and pray for these. After an hour or so, we would look at the list to see what we still wanted to pray for, leaving the rest till next week. We would be totally free to skip to other topics that came to mind, while using our own style. Sometimes, we would have a small tea break. In all this, it is good to remember to pray from a cleansed heart, so that He can hear our prayers.

Group discussion and prayer:
1. Do you pray mostly for the truly big issues, or for some small things, too?
2. A prayer life as natural as breathing - how would you achieve that, amidst all the daily chores and a busy lifestyle?
3. Could you tell something about answered prayer?

3 Strive for deep obedience to the Lord, also in your thought life

Obedience in our thoughts is one of the important keys to renewal (Jhn.14:15-18; 1.Jhn.5:9; Rom.12:1-2). We can always ask ourselves, "What is it that God *really* wants of me?" We can let all our desires be directed to making His heart rejoice and to do things out of love for Him, whatever the costs and circumstances. This is in itself a simple choice but it can be hard to do! Yet only from our deepening relationship with the Lord Jesus can we truly bear lasting fruit (Jhn.15:5-16). If we want to "abide in Him" it helps us to make sure that no sin (in word, deed, or even thoughts!) is between us and the Lord: by confessing it silently as soon as we notice it, and by keeping it at a distance. For it does not belong to us as children of the King! It is good and right to come to the Lord for forgiveness repeatedly throughout the day - He looks at our heart and loves us, and is so happy if we come (Jhn.6:37; 7:37). Even like the prodigal son we may consciously accept His forgiveness, for He truly does forgive like no man ever can. That means the end of all our feelings of guilt and shame, and the basis of our victory ground! That way, we also close the door to the enemy, who wants to harass us with his accusations or have a claim on our lives through the door of not yet forgiven sins.

A practical example: unclean thoughts

If we have a problem with unclean thoughts - whenever we notice one - it is best to bring this thought to the Lord immediately and ask for His forgiveness (Ch.9(2,3)). Then: do accept that precious forgiveness and thank Him for it. It is so easy to "go through the motions" without truly accepting His forgiveness and knowing that He has cleansed our heart, so that we need no longer condemn ourselves. We may always come to Him for forgiveness.

Some of us are tempted easily (Jam.1:12-15; 2.Pet.2:7-9). Men may need to be very careful where they "put their eyes" (a choice that can grow into a good habit); the ladies may need to be aware that feelings can be very unrealistic and are not something to be directed by. When unclean thoughts have become habitual, we may have to go to Him very frequently (a speedy prayer with open eyes when we are at work, a longer prayer perhaps in the evening); but do keep coming to Him, as that is what He intends for us (Mt.11:28-30; Jam.4:8; Ps.69:18-19). He hates sin but loves to see us repent and come into His presence, which truly also is a place of healing and safety.

On our part, there are also things we need to do. Never forget that we are in battle against a dangerous enemy! To win the war, we must close the door of our heart to the evil one who seeks to force himself in through dirty jokes, wrong TV-programs, filthy magazines etc. What would you do if a lion jumps towards you - fight him single-handedly? Or flee for safety to the nearby shelter? God is our refuge (Ps.46). He is ready to protect us, and He is the Almighty. Perhaps we try to fight our own unsuccessful battles, especially in the realm of our thoughts. For believe me, you will lose - the enemy is very real and very powerful. The more we fight problems in our own strength, the more we think about these, which - although differently - still keeps such unclean thoughts in focus. They are wrong company. Let's turn our back on them and our face towards God, as we pray for forgiveness and then for the Holy Spirit to help us. Let Him be our focus! Philippians 4:8-9 has such lovely advice for us...

Wounds that we keep clean heal more quickly. A way of prevention is, to bring the many old sins in this realm to Him for forgiveness, to throw out wrong magazines and books, to stop looking at wrong TV-programs (it helps not to look at all) - bringing to the Lord even the memories of old films and fantasies and events. Make sure to accept His forgiveness for these, and see to it that you have forgiven others who may have played a role in these matters... If even the small sins of the past (in as far as we remember these) have been brought to Him, the enemy may find no backdoors left by which to mess up our lives. Moreover, it's then as if we have more freedom to focus on whatever is good. Should we be attacked again, then the victory seems easier. When the enemy finds no old sins in our heart to hold on to, but Jesus instead, that place becomes uncomfortable to him.

Do not be discouraged if you fall back, just remain close to Him and ask for His forgiveness (read Col.1:13-14, 2.Cor.5:16-18). Remember, you are child of the King, and He wants to live in your heart! And if, sometimes, we are harassed with images that have truly left a mark on our thoughts, we may ask Him to *cleanse* us of all unrighteousness (1.Jhn.1:9). We can then pray, for instance, "Lord, I keep remembering that terrible movie. Will You forgive me for seeing it, and for harbouring those unclean memories in my thoughts? Please, Lord, also cleanse me of these, and help me to focus my thoughts on pure things. Thank You, that You have forgiven me. Amen."

Proverbs 4:23 says that we are to guard our heart above all else, for from it flows the wellspring of our very life. Therefore, let's guard the world of our thoughts and memories. Let us fill what space we still have left - even as we get older - with pure and loving thoughts as we ask the Holy Spirit to help us, with forgiving and helping others, with reading the Word of God and seeking His presence, with listening to songs of praise. That works two ways, as it also fills up our "thought library" with good things and forms different, delightful habits!

Still, (perhaps through old habit) a wrong thought may come up occasionally. Then remember that we cannot always prevent a thought from coming up, but we can stop thinking it through as we cast ourselves upon the Lord. Yet this shows that it's worth it to occasionally have a close look at the "library of our memory" to see if dirty stuff has truly been cast out as we ask and receive God's forgiveness. Our fantasy can then more easily dwell on good things with which to fill our hearts.

During this battle of faith, we can rejoice in God's mercy and remain close to Him. If at times we are much tempted in our thoughts, get busy in a practical way: do dishes, write those long over-due letters, mow the lawn - and you will feel good instead of bad. It also helps to promise ourselves something when we have reached a goal we set ourselves in not dwelling on unclean thoughts when they present themselves to us for - say - a month or more. We may then, for instance, promise ourselves to purchase a beautiful book we want, as a special encouragement.

In battle we become stronger, as we learn to live by the much-needed grace of God, to truly accept His forgiveness because Jesus paid the price for our sins - sins that did hurt the heart of God who loves us. Isn't it wonderful that our redemption, righteousness, and holiness are in Jesus (1.Cor.1:27-31, 6:9-11). There is true salvation for *all* of us (Jhn.6:35-37, 7:37).

Important: Our battle of faith may be in a totally different area - yet often it also begins in our thoughts. We can use our spiritual armour (Gal.6:10-18) and the example of "how to deal with uncleanness" above to also tackle that different realm of sin; perhaps bitterness, jealousy, or an unforgiving heart. This may give us some home work to do...

Group discussion and prayer:
1. Can you mention an experience in which you were obedient even though it meant a battle of faith?
2. Are there any areas of life where you find it hard to obey, and why?
3. How do you tackle wrong thoughts?

4 Ask the Lord right away to forgive you if you sin. Also, forgive yourself and learn to love yourself.

When we get used to asking forgiveness right after we have sinned, this will soon become a good habit. As we consciously ask the Lord for His forgiveness, not just confessing the sin, it is so wonderful to realize that we are cleansed by Him, standing before God without reproach. Whenever we have repented from sin, it helps to once again ask for the power of the Holy Spirit (we cannot keep our path clean in our own strength). I once knew a young man who always did this whenever he had brought his sins to the Lord Jesus. Although he did not have much insight in Who the Holy Spirit was, the "fragrance of the Lord" (2.Cor.2:14-16) and the fruit of the Holy Spirit started to become visible in his life! We may ask the Holy Spirit to enter those newly washed areas in our life.

Once you know that your conscience has been cleansed from guilt, it is easier to love the Lord and to love yourself as well. He took upon Himself your sinful load because He loved you - you are loveable in His eyes. He knows you personally and intimately; he now restores your self-respect in that he has cleansed you - for we may also forgive and love ourselves, as He has done. The way to God is open, we can bring our prayers to Him with renewed authority - not based on our hard work but on the fact that He cleansed us...

Hidden sins, therefore, hurt us more than we think. They hinder our prayers and relationship with God, they keep the door open to the accuser. They rob us of our self-respect - they rob it more than any self-respect we fear to lose in confessing our sins! Un-confessed sins also rob us of our authority and joy; they can even generate new sins (covering the old ones up, or simply continuing with those sins and creating a habit). What a relief it brings to know that our sins are forgiven, that all things have become new... (Eze.36:26; Rev.21:5).

Most of us are not so used to forgiving and loving ourselves (we have fallen so often). Nevertheless, Jesus does - and so may (must!) we. Why let the accuser have his way, to keep pointing us to sins already forgiven? It is so important to *keep choosing* to accept the Lord's forgiveness. Accept it in faith (1.Jhn.1:9; Jhn.3:16-17; Ac.5:31). As we learn to accept and love ourselves, we also learn to forgive and love the other person. We cannot truly love and respect others more than we love ourselves; and many of us who cannot love have never learned to love themselves, and to be happy with who God made them. Realizing this will soften our heart also towards difficult people. They are mostly people with a problem. If we have learned to love ourselves (see also Ch.5) and to see ourselves more like our loving God sees us - and that is mostly quite different from the way the world sees us - we will also see the other person more from God's loving perspective! Through our own experiences we can then understand them in their battles, and stand next to them in love (Mk.12:31-33; Jhn.13:34-35; Rom.13:8-10; 1.Cor.13:4-7). In other words: through our own love relationship with God it becomes easier to love them and to help them find the foundation for their life in what the Lord Jesus can do for them, too.

The lovely thing is, that as we keep learning more to forgive ourselves, realizing that Jesus' blood has cleansed us, we learn to appreciate and esteem ourselves. We will then see not only ourselves but also others with different eyes (Mat.5:8). "Something lives in every hue, Christless eyes have never seen", as an old hymn says. As it then becomes easier to forgive, love and esteem others, they in turn can start appreciating us more! It radiates from us, so to speak, improving the atmosphere - even though they may not yet know the secret of the power we find in our relationship with the Lord Jesus Christ.

Group discussion and prayer:
1. Why can we truly love ourselves - isn't that pride? Do we love ourselves, just as God does?
2. Do you know if all of your sins have been forgiven?
3. Do you regularly pray for the power and help of the Holy Spirit? What do you know about Him?

5 Develop a lifestyle of forgiveness towards all people that you come across

The Bible has a lot to say about forgiving others (e.g. Mt.6:14-15; 18:35; Eph.4:31-32). Allow no bitterness into your thoughts. Should it already be there because of past events, then immediately start forgiving all those involved thoroughly in your heart - with a choice of your will, even though your feelings may still hurt. Wounds do take time to heal, and with some deeply seated feelings of pain and bitterness it may be necessary to repeatedly forgive, also as such an event may have different aspects which we remember only later on; or if that deeply seated bitterness has not quite vanished yet. In many situations, it can come back even though our decision to forgive was complete - then renew your decision to forgive that person in your heart and pray for him or her, that God will bless them and reveal Himself to them. Perhaps, we only seek the guilt within ourselves in a painful event; we ask God's forgiveness and yet the pain seems to remain. Then, it may help to dare have an objective look - perhaps the other person was (also) wrong? God cannot forgive us for things we have not even done. Moreover, he cannot forgive us for things we *did* do, if we will not forgive others who sinned against us (Mt.6:12-15; Mk.11:24-26). Do not hesitate to even forgive the other person if they have committed some very real sins - for where no real sins were committed, our forgiveness may not really be needed.

Perhaps the other person is not yet ready to discuss the issue at stake - perhaps they need to speak about it and forgive us for the sins they see in us, yet dare not tell us so. *If at all possible, it is good to keep the lines of communication open to him or her and prayerfully talk to them about it.* (Ch.8(9)) It will be harder for us to speak the truth than to keep avoiding the person and the issue. But: it may be so necessary! (1.Jhn.4:20-21; Mt.5:23-24) That means: taking a risk, dying to your image or prestige, admitting your own guilt if confronted. It pleases God if relationships are restored, and it helps the other person as well as ourselves to get rid of any reasons for bitterness - being a friend to them instead. Sometimes, we may not have the confidence to do so; it then helps to ask for advice and prayer with those we can truly trust and who know how to keep a secret (also for the sake of the other person). If it appears that the other person is not open to talk (or he/she does not want to forgive), we may wait for a better time in an attitude of forgiveness - by all means, allow no bitterness into your heart! Just hand over the person and all the problems into God's care; He wants to be their Shepherd, too. Having done all that is in your power, and with the certainty of a pure heart, give it all back to the Lord. He may also use others to reach out to this person.

Forgiving others can be an important key in the healing of our own hurting feelings, as well as in the restoration of relationships. Moreover, it is a powerful stimulus for intercessory prayer. We can do our best to choose with our whole will (the heart mostly follows only later) to love the other person, to forgive and to serve him or her in practical ways. Loving others does not always mean that they are loveable, but it does mean that we strive to attain what is best for them and feel responsible for their welfare. We can do so by prayer, by helping them when needed, by standing next to them and their relatives where we can. We cannot do so in our own strength, but from our relationship with the Lord and out of the safety we experience with Him. By handing out Jesus' love we make His heart rejoice, especially when it costs us something...

Group discussion and prayer:
1. Forgiving - in what way? Do you know of any practical steps that helped you?

2. Can you forgive others, even if they do not ask you to, and if they have forgotten their wrongdoings or are not wanting to face them?
3. Are there people in your past who wronged you and whom you have not yet forgiven?

6 Make sure your relationships are in order, in as far as it depends on you

This is something we can really work towards. We find many guidelines about this in the Bible (Rom.12:17-21; Mt.5:43-48; Luk.6:27-31), and can do our utmost to keep our relationships right - blessing and helping them where we can. It helps to approach them with an open heart, even though we are then vulnerable. It is also important to be a blessing to others, especially to those who are not appreciated, as there is a special secret hidden there (Mt.25:40). We can even hang the "Golden Rule" (Mt.7:12) above our pillow! Give to others what you would want for yourself if you were in his or her shoes - it helps to think about their situation and problems, not simply of our own, if we want to understand them.

As a young Christian, I used to say, "Lord, I don't hate anybody" - but that was not enough... He want us to actively love others. It is not just necessary to keep others out of harm, but on the contrary to do them good, even to your enemies. That way, we learn to take their feelings into account, and to help them out of our own experiences in life. For instance, we can see more easily if the other person is lonely when we have gone through hurtful times of loneliness ourselves, and are then more quickly motivated to help him or her. That may cost us something: in popularity, in chances that we then may miss for ourselves - or we may feel it in our purse. But if we have asked for God's guidance in this, we may know that in our sacrifice His loving eye is upon us, and that He will use the situation to bring good out of it (Rom.8:28).

We can learn to give love without asking anything back, to be lowly like Jesus (Jhn.13:3-5; Php.2:5-8). That means:

to lose your life, to take up your cross and follow Jesus. In our former lives we chose for success, esteem, possessions, striving to be the best. But in our life with Jesus we will learn to choose to esteem others higher than ourselves, to humble ourselves, to confess our sins, to serve and to wash the feet of others. Also, in our relationship with God we learn to obey Him more than people; to forgive others, to be unselfish and patient, even as we relate to those with differing opinions or a difficult character. Let us not answer darkness with darkness, but be a light in it and bring change. Our glory will not come from men but from God, Who sees our innermost being, giving us a deep joy out of our relationship with Him (Ps.16:5-11).

Group discussion and prayer:
1. What does the "Golden Rule" mean to you? How would you like to be treated by others? Are you already doing that for others?
2. Are there any relationships in your life that you find difficult to cope with?

7 Overcome that which is evil by doing what is good

This is no easy task, and we can ask for the help and strength of the Holy Spirit. Many books have been written on this, and here we will just mention the importance of regularly asking the Holy Spirit to fill us with God's love and power, even if we have received the "baptism of the Holy Spirit" in the past. Fruit from our life does not come by our own efforts, but by being close to Jesus and by the power of His Holy Spirit (Jhn.15:1-6; Gal.5:22). Martin Luther had Acts 1:8 inscribed on his desk as his favorite verse, and such was the influence of this imperfect man that he has been called the "Man of the Millennium"!

When we act in the "opposite spirit" by serving others and giving instead of just receiving, we can be like a light in the darkness (Rom.12:20-21; Luk.6:27; Jam.4:17; 1.Cor.13:4-7; 1.Pet.4:11). This means: focusing on whatever is good around us, being positive towards others and building them up when we speak - even though we may disagree with some of their opinions. That becomes easier as we leave the judging to God and the grudging to the enemy; as we learn to bless others in our heart, especially when the relationship is difficult. Prayer changes things! By love, we can break through the resistance or through the mask behind which the other person may hide.

Love does not always come naturally, especially in an environment where there is disagreement, sinful behaviour, nasty words - it is there we need to make a choice with our will. Love is not unrealistic; it acts from a God-given grace (Rom.5:5). We need to pray for that grace, for His love to work through us when we find nothing within ourselves. Responding to darkness with more darkness (our bitterness, lack of forgiveness) will not help the situation but rather make it worse; yet our God-given love is like a light that shines in the darkness, and darkness can do nothing against it (Jhn.1:4-14). If a room is dark and we switch on the light (it does not happen by itself, we need to decide to move that switch) then the darkness will absolutely disappear. It cannot overcome the light - simply because the light is more powerful! The light God has given to His children is like a reflection of His glory (2.Cor.3:18; 4:6-9; Ps.16:5-11; 1.Pet.4:13-14), and we can receive it by spending time with Him. If we keep focussing on the darkness and worry about all its aspects (I sometimes tend to do this), our faces will darken; yet if we start focussing on the Lord and His glory, we will change and reflect Him, and then have something to give to the dark world around us.

As we learn to respond in the "opposite spirit" (Ch.3(9), 8(7)), we also learn to pray for the empowering and help of the Holy Spirit. It is always good to ask God to give us more of His Holy Spirit - a Spirit of prayer, not of criticism; of love, not of fear (2.Tim.1:7); of selflessness, not of self-centredness. Therefore, when we meet negative situations and difficult people, *it is important to consider what good things are lacking*! This is where we can add what lacks - by the example of our own life and out of God's empowering. He is the great Counselor and Comforter; He is always so near and willing to guide us. We can always come to Him and ask for more of the Holy Spirit when we cannot handle things ourselves. Let us just be open to His work in our life, so that His beautiful fruit may grow in us (Gal.5:22-23). That way, we learn to place the other person first, and that it is more blessed to give than to receive! Just try it - it may surprise you...

Group discussion and prayer:
1. Have you ever overcome evil with good in your life? Can you give an example of that?
2. Can you think of some present situations where you could apply this?

8 Hold on to the truth of Gods Word, whatever your feelings may tell you

The truth is, that God deeply loves you and that He has a solution for your need. You can hold on to the truth of His Word (Jhn.8:31-32; Mt.28:20)! As we yield to Him in prayer, He comforts us by His presence. Yet often we are so busy or our emotions can be so shaken, that we do not sense His comfort - then know that His Word is the unfailing truth whatever our feelings make us believe... Our feelings can be impaired by events from the past, making us believe that we are unloved, that the situation is hopelessness anyway, that God is far away and does not care, etc. Then hold on to God's Word as an anchor for your soul (Hebr.6:17-20) and as a guideline - place it above your feelings! (Ch.9(4)). This is very important. Our feelings are not always the truth - God's Word *is*. We often need a firm choice of our will to place God's thoughts above our own thoughts and emotions, but it is so important. That way, we make a straight path before our feet (Hebr.12:12-13).

It helps to regularly read and study the Bible - it is a lamp for our feet as we walk the path of life (Ps.119:105). The righteous do not live by feelings, but by *faith* (Hab.2:4; Rom.1:17; Gal.3:11; Hebr.10:38). Faith is simply: handing ourselves over to God (feelings and all), and acting upon what His Word says. It has a lot to do with faithfulness. We do not need to understand everything in the Bible or have some special feelings, to do what it says. As you sit down for your daily Bible reading, just ask yourself if there is anything that can be applied practically in your life, and then start working on that consciously. If certain things take extra effort, it can be a real help to learn a Bible verse on that by heart - at unexpected moments, we can then remind ourselves of it.

Using a concordance can be tremendously useful in whatever our circumstances. It helps to look up words that relate to your situation - what you are missing in it, or what you would like to attain: such as joy, salvation, power, heaven, patience. This can bring unexpected surprises and answers, and this method has often helped and blessed me.

Make sure to test your feelings to the *truth*: the truth of God's Word, but also the truth of things as they really happened. Sometimes, we may too quickly draw conclusions from the circumstances, without knowing all the facts. What do we do if an acquaintance does not greet us or looks bad tempered - do we then immediately think: there is some disagreement, I must have caused it, our relationship is over, shall I ever dare greet him again, etc. (you may recognize this). Are our thoughts in touch with reality as God sees it? Perhaps the other person was just deep in thought; maybe he has problems or just a sad day. Or perhaps he is so tired that he closes himself to things around him for a while. He may badly need "the benefit of the doubt". If we harbour unhealthy conclusions, this can influence our future relationship; therefore, it is better to work on forgiving and loving that person and to bring him or her before the throne of God in prayer. In the end, each person is sensitive to real love; it is one of the mightiest weapons we have as Christians (1.Cor.13:13).

Finally: Jesus said of Himself that He is the truth (Jhn.14:6). How remarkable that, in the deepest sense, the truth is a Person - One who died and rose from the grave; One we can come to know; One Who loves us and guides us into all truth by His Holy Spirit (Jhn.16:13). He will help us to make a right path both for our feet and our thoughts.

Group discussion and prayer:
1. What does your mind tell you about God, and what do your feelings say? What are the points of difference?
2. How can we maintain a truthful thought life?

9 Count your blessings - make a list of them!

It helps to closely notice the good things in our own life. Those, too, are truth in spite of difficult circumstances (the banner of the cross that we carry in a dark world). We can focus on a continuous gratitude to the Lord. There will always be something we can thank Him for: His love for us, the beauty of creation around us, His special gifts and possibilities in us - in short: counting our blessings! The choice is ours: if we pay much attention to this, the blessings find more room in our heart and circumstances can get a different perspective.

One of the best ways to really "count" is by making a list of God's blessings in our life. It helps us to sit down with a pen, spend time with Him, and thank Him whenever something comes to mind that we can thank Him for. That brings our situation into His perspective - with Him, there is always so much hope, in spite of the very imperfect world around us.

It has helped me to have a "history notebook" (Mal.3:16) - one in which I write down things He seems to say to me, or things that happened in which He acted, even through the years, as a precious memory. The Bible would not have been written if people in Old Testament times had not wanted to remember the mighty acts of God. We may believe we will always remember - but memories do fade with time, and writing them down will encourage us in the future. It will uplift us to reread what God has spoken or done in similar situations in our life, when at times we may feel sad.

In such a notebook, there can also be a place for the things God teaches us in a certain situation. Guard His precious wisdom in your life. This present book has partly been a result of such notes over the years. You may help others with what you have learned in your own life - such wisdom is far more powerful than wisdom people just read about!

Friends are a blessing, too. It will help you to see your own blessings if you count those of others: "she is a very faithful person, has been educated by wise parents, she is always open to help, or a good cook". What do others see in *us*? That is a precious addition to our own list...

Group discussion and prayer:
1. Can you share something good that God has spoken or done for you recently?
2. Would you like prayer for situations that make it hard to count your blessings?
3. Write down good qualities in others that are a blessing to those around them, for each person in the group. Bring these along to the next group meeting and share them.

10 Do not hesitate to ask a trustworthy Christian friend for prayer and advice

Asking for help is not easy. If we can go to friends that can keep a secret or to a prayer group in church, this can make things less heavy - they know us, appreciate us. It is not always wise to tell those in our group all the details of our situation (especially when these can be too difficult for them to handle, or puts the people involved in a bad light), but it can be quite a help if we ask our friends or group to pray for us.

Because of their life experience, other Christians are sometimes wiser than we think. We may learn from them - think of dedicated Christians that you respect. Perhaps there is a well-trusted deacon or pastor in your church, whom you can ask in private for help or prayer.

Sometimes, the pain may be very deep, and we do not seem to get over it. Some situations may be hard for others to understand or handle, especially the more difficult situations in life. Then it can be quite important to find a good Christian counselor to help us - a pastor, psychiatrist, marriage counselor etc. It can be wise to find such professional help. Do not let the situation crush you - God wants you to receive help, to make you whole and to bless you. Hold on to the Good Shepherd Who walks next to you – God is our Refuge, He is always there for you (Ps.46).

Those among us who have gone through trials ourselves may be able to help those who go through similar experiences. We can then speak from experience. If helping others comes naturally, if we have compassion for others, if we have learned to listen, or if people seek us out for advice and counsel, it may be good to pray if God wants to use us in this area. We can then consider reading some helpful pastoral books or doing a good course.

Group discussion and prayer:
1. What do you believe are the kind of situations where we need help of mature Christians, or where would professional help be the best choice?
2. What do you think are the qualities of a good counselor?
3. Would you be able to give good advice and counsel to others?

TOPICAL REGISTER

Subject:	Chapter:
Abilities	5(4; 6)
Abundance	1(2)
Acceptance	2(6); 4(5,7); 5(1,3)
Accusations	1(1,2); 2(6); 4(2); 8(2,9)
Advice	2(13); 3(4); App.10
Anger	2(8)
Appearance	5(6)
Appreciation	4(7); 5(1,8)
Attitude	8(6,7,11); 9(9)
Authority	9(3); App.4
Bible	1(3); 3(7); 5(1); 9(4,6); App.8
Blessings, counting	2(5); App.9
Book of Remembrance	1(3); 2(5); App.9
Causes, finding	2(8); 4(6)
Character	3(8); 9(8)
Change	3(1); 9
Choices	8(3,10,11); 9(8)
Comforted by God	1(3,4,5); 7(4)
Comforting others	1(10); 4(9)
Communicating	2(9); 8(9,10)
Comparison with others	5(1,2)
Confrontation	2(8); 8(1,9)
Contact with others	2(11); 7
Convictions	3(7)
Counseling	2(13); 3(4); App.10
Courage	4(8); 5(4)
Creativity	5(7); 6(5)
Criticism	3(3); 8(1,2,5)
Dependence	3(2)
Depression	2(13)
Difficult days	1(8); 2(8,12)
Discouragement	2
Encouraging others	4(9); 5(8); 6(7)

Enemies	8(6,7)
Expectations	4
Face the facts	1(6); 3(5); 5(5)
False humility	5(4)
Fear of man	3; 5(4)
Feelings, led by	4(2,6); 5(3,5); 9(4); App.8
"First love"	2(2); 3(1); 4(1); 5(2,3); 7(3); App.1
Forgiveness of sins	1(1,2); 7(2); 8(2); 9(2,4); App.4
Forgiving others	1(9); 3(3); 4(6); 7(2); 8(2,3); 9(3,4,8); App.5
Forgiving yourself	App.4
Friendship	1(10); 3(9); 7(5,6); 8(10)
Fruit	1(9); 4(5)
Gloom	2
Goals	2(7); 3(1,2); 4(5); 6(4,6)
Golden Rule	6(2); 7(6); 8(11); App.6
Goodness of God	1(2); 2(1); 5(3); 9(4,5)
Grace	6(3)
Group discussions	Appendix
Growth	1(9); 4(4); 7(3)
Guidance	4(3); 6(2,3,4); 7(5)
Guilt	1(1,2); 2(8); 4(2); 8(2); App.4
Happiness	2(7); 7(3); App.1
Healthy lifestyle	2(11)
Heart direction	3(1)
Helping others	1(10); 3(9); 4(9); 5(8); 6(7); 7(9)
Holiness	1(2)
Honoring the Lord	1(8)
Holy Spirit	3(8); 4(8); 6(2,5); 7(4); 8(2); 9(7); App.7
Hope	1(2,5); 2(1)
Humility	5(4)
Ideals	6(5,6)
Identity	2(6); 3(8); 4(3); 5(4); 6
Idols	3(2)
"In Christ"	2(6); 4(2)
Influence on others	9(9)
Insecurity	4
Instrument of God	6(2,5)
Inviting Jesus	1(5)

Jealousy	5(2)
Joy	1(7)
Lesson in Lebanon	5(3)
Letters	8(9)
Limitations	2(8)
Listening	7(6); App.10
Loneliness	2(8); 3(6); 7
Loving others	1(10); 3(9); 7(6); 8(5)
Loving yourself	4(5,7); 5(2,5)
Maturity	4(4)
Mirror	8(5)
New creation	1(2); 2(6); 4(2)
Obedience	1(9); 3(7,9); App.3
Openness	7(7,8); 8(1,3)
Opinion	4(3,4)
Opposite spirit	3(9); 8(5,7); 9(9); App.7
Passivity	5(4)
Peace makers	8(11)
Perfectionism	4(5)
Performance orientation	4(5); 5(1,7); 6(1)
Plan for our life	2(7); 6(4)
Pleasing people	3(6)
"Positive thinking"	5(5)
Praise	1(8); 2(4)
Prayer	1(9); 2(3); 3(4); 4(3,6); 8(6,7); App.2
Presence of the Lord	1(4,5); 2(2)
Pride	5(4)
Rejection	7(2)
Relationship with God	4(1); 6(3); 7(1,3); App.1
Relationship with others	7; 8; App.6
Renewal	9
Rest	2(8,11)
Restoration	7(5); 8; App.6
Security	1(9); 4(1,2)
Self-acceptance	5(1)
Self-assurance	4
Self-esteem	3(2); 4(7); App.4
Self-image	4(6); 5; 6(1)
Self-pity	2(9)
Self-sufficiency	4(3); 5(1,2)

Shyness	3; 4(4,8)
Slander	3(5); 6(2); 8(8)
Sorrow	1(5)
Spiritual gifts	6(4); 9(7)
Strength	1(9)
Stress	2(8)
Suffering	1
Teaspoon, example of	6(5)
Thought patterns	3(7); 5(5); 6(3); 8(8); 9; App.3
Time well-spent	1(9); 2(12); 7(3)
Truth vs. lies	5(3,5); 6(3); 8(5); 9(4); App.8
Unclean thoughts	9(2,3); App.3
Valley	2(1,7)
Victory	1(1,2); 9; App.3
Worrying	2(10)
Worship	2(4); 9(5).

RECOMMENDED BOOKS

Paul E. Billheimer, *"Don't Waste Your Sorrows"*, Christian Literature Crusade, Inc., Fort Washington (1977); ISBN 0-90028-453-6.

Leanne Payne, *Real Presence. The Holy Spirit in the Works of C.S. Lewis"*, Crossway Books, Westchester, Illinois 60153, USA (1979); ISBN 0-89107-164-4.

William & Candace Backus, *"Untwisting Twisted Relationships. How to Restore Close Ties With Family and Friends"*, Bethany House Publ., Minneapolis, Minnesota 55438, USA (1988); ISBN 0-87123-998-1.

William Backus & Marie Chapian, *"Telling Yourself the Truth"*, Bethany House Publ., Minneapolis, Minnesota 55438, USA (19..); ISBN ...

Cecil G. Osborn, *"The Art of Learning to Love Yourself"*, The Zondervan Corp., Grand Rapids, Michigan 49506, USA (1976); ISBN 0-310-30572-1.

David Augsburger, *"Caring Enough to Confront"*, Regal Books, ... (Rev.ed. 1981), ISBN...

Bruce & Barbara Thompson, *"Walls of My Heart. Powerful Keys to Breaking Out and Being Free"*, Crown Ministries Int., P.O.Box 49, Euclid, Minnesota 56722, USA (1989); ISBN 0-935779-13-2.

Graham Powell, *"Fear Free"*, Sovereign World Ltd., P.O.Box 17, Chichester, PO20 6RY, England (1987); ISBN 1-85240-015-3.

Don Baker & Emery Nester, *"Depression. Finding Hope & Meaning in Life's Darkest Shadow"*, Multnomah Press, Portland, Oregon 97266, USA (1983); ISBN 0-88070-186-2.

J. Oswald Sanders, *"Facing Loneliness. The Starting Point of a New Journey"*, Highland Books, Broadway House, Crowborough, TN6 1BY, England (1988); ISBN 0-946616-48-5.

Ralph Mattson & Arthur Miller, *"Finding a Job You can Love"*, Thomas Nelson Publ., Nashville-Camden-New York, USA (1982); ISBN 0-8407-5817-0.

John & Paula Sandford, *"The Transformation of the Inner Man"*, Victory House, Tulsa, Oklahoma 74136, USA (1982); ISBN 0-932081-13-4.

John & Paula Sandford, *"Healing the Wounded Spirit"*, Bridge Publishing, Inc., South Plainfield, NJ 07080 (1985); ISBN 0-88270-591-1; and some of their other books.

Floyd McClung Jr., *"The Fatherheart of God"*; Harvest House Publishers (2004), ISBN 0-736912-15-0

David A. Seamands, *"Healing for Damaged Emotions"*, Scripture Press, Victor Books, USA (1981); ISBN 90-6067-235-6 (?); and some of his other books.

On the Road to Renewal

08W11336